Bound 1970

THE ROLE OF IDEOLOGY
IN THE AMERICAN REVOLUTION

THE ROLE OF IDEOLOGY IN THE AMERICAN REVOLUTION

Edited by **JOHN R. HOWE, JR.**
University of Minnesota

HOLT, RINEHART AND WINSTON
New York · Chicago · San Francisco · Atlanta
Dallas · Montreal · Toronto · London · Sydney

Cover illustration: "Zion Besieged and Attacked." Detail
of a cartoon, 1787, dealing with the proposed attack on
the Pennsylvania state constitution by bankers and vested
interests. *(Free Public Library of Philadelphia)*

Copyright © 1970 by Holt, Rinehart and Winston, Inc.
All Rights Reserved
Library of Congress Catalog Card Number: 70–104813
SBN: 03–077800–X
Printed in the United States of America
9   8   7   6   5   4   3   2   1

CONTENTS

COMMON SENSE;

ADDRESSED TO THE

INHABITANTS

OF

AMERICA,

On the following interesting

SUBJECTS.

I. Of the Origin and Defign of Government in general, with concife Remarks on the Englifh Conftitution.

II. Of Monarchy and Hereditary Succeffion.

III. Thoughts on the prefent State of American Affairs.

IV. Of the prefent Ability of America, with fome mifcellaneous Reflections.

A NEW EDITION, with feveral Additions in the Body of the Work. To which is added an APPENDIX; together with an Addrefs to the People called QUAKERS.

N. B. The New Addition here given increafes the Work upwards of one Third.

Man knows no Mafter fave creating HEAVEN,
Or thofe whom Choice and common Good ordain.
THOMSON.

PHILADELPHIA PRINTED.

And SOLD by W. and T. BRADFORD.

Title page of *Common Sense*, pamphlet by Thomas Paine, 1776. *(New York Public Library)*

INTRODUCTION

What was the American Revolution? Americans of the eighteenth century, confronted with the tasks of revolution making and nation building, asked the question, and students of the Revolutionary Era have continued to debate it ever since.

Certain things are, of course, clear. Thirteen of England's North American colonies declared their independence and combined, however imperfectly, into a new nation. But beyond this what happened? Was the Revolution essentially a war for national independence, prosecuted against an "outside" colonial power much in the manner of twentieth-century colonial rebellions? Or did the period from the 1760s to the 1780s bring as well a basic restructuring of colonial society? If so, how radical were the internal consequences of the revolutionary experience and which areas of colonial life and thought were most profoundly affected? Again, were such changes central to the original revolutionary impulse, or were they largely unanticipated, a by-product of the fundamental contest with England? These are the basic problems that have confronted students of the American Revolution from the eighteenth century to the twentieth. Anyone intending to understand the Revolutionary Era must somehow come directly to grips with them.

During the nineteenth century, historians focused their attention on the democratic and nationalistic aspects of the revolutionary experience. The principles of liberty and democracy that guided the colonists in their struggle against England and the sense of common national identity that resulted from it were what impressed them most about the Revolution.

In the first half of the twentieth century the main emphasis of Revolutionary scholarship shifted. Historians seemed more concerned with the disagreements among the revolutionary generation over matters of social and political philosophy and with the internal conflicts to which these disagreements led. As a consequence, books and articles appeared detailing the battles between "radicals" and "conservatives" and the sudden democratization of the political order that followed: extension of the franchise to a formerly disenfranchised majority, the opening of political office to men formerly excluded, and the replacement of a dominant elite by a democratic majority. Scholars emphasized as well the revolutionary (read democratic) impact of independence and war upon the social structure: the exodus of

1

Tories, largely from the upper class; the sale and widespread redistribution of confiscated Tory property; the severing of traditional ties between church and state; the questioning and weakening of Negro chattel slavery.

More recently still, students of the Revolution have presented major challenges to this concept of the "internal revolution." A flood of scholarly writing has emerged advancing the view that colonial society was remarkably democratic even before the Revolution and that such social institutions as class structure, patterns of landholding, and church-state relations were but marginally influenced by the tide of revolutionary events. To be sure, certain localities were severely disrupted by the exodus of Tory elements and the economic dislocations generated by withdrawal from the British empire and the long and costly war. But it now seems difficult to perceive any large-scale internal revolution accompanying the colonial break with England.

In the area of political life more impressive and far-reaching changes do seem to have occurred. Consider the following: the heated debate about natural rights and the dangers of tyrannical power; the political activism generated in the course of framing protests against England and constructing new governments once independence had been declared; the experience of employing extralegal county, state, and national conventions to challenge and ultimately overthrow constituted authority; the vastly expanded opportunities for political career building which these conditions provided. All these factors worked upon American political life in unsettling and disruptive ways, radicalizing institutions and modes of behavior and leaving them significantly changed. These, it now appears, were the areas of experience that underwent some of the most profound alteration.

Yet even here the case for a thoroughgoing revolution is not easily made. Much recent scholarship has shown rather convincingly that the political struggle between radicals and conservatives within the several states was neither as sharp nor as pervasive as was formerly believed; that in many areas the majority of white adult males could vote well before the Revolution; and that political leadership, at least as compared with that of most of the other great modern revolutions, was remarkably continuous throughout the Revolutionary period.

If, then, the American Revolution was moderate in its social dimensions and if it proved less than fully revolutionary even in its political aspects, does this mean that there was nothing radical, nothing truly revolutionary about it? In trying to arrive at an acceptable answer to this basic question, scholars have most recently turned with increasing interest to still another area of experience, that of revolutionary ideology. The present volume is designed to explore this particular subject.

The selections that follow should be read with two groups of questions clearly in mind. The first has to do with the content and character of revolutionary political thought. How radical or conservative was it in terms of its democratic content? Was it fresh and creative or simply an extension of earlier colonial intellectual traditions? Did the revolutionary generation in fact develop anything that can be called an ideology; that is, a comprehensive and well-integrated system of belief? Or do we find something considerably less rigorous and systematic, little more than a miscellaneous gathering of essentially unrelated thoughts? Finally, can one talk about "the" revolutionary ideology or were there several? That is, what impresses most, the broad areas of agreement among revolutionary writers or the differences among them in value, belief, and policy?

The second group of questions has to do generally with the role, or function, of political ideology during the Revolutionary Era. Some writers contend that for the men of the revolutionary generation ideology was a rationalization for behavior determined largely by nonideological factors such as economic interest or political ambition. Others insist that revolutionary leaders viewed the world about them through the prism of political theory and acted consciously on behalf of principles and belief. The reader will want to make his own judgments about this and also, perhaps, about the broader question of whether ideas are likely to influence men's actions more at some times, and under some conditions, than at others.

Again, what can be determined about the relationship between ideology and its social and political context in revolutionary America? Some of the selections in this volume suggest that radical advances took place first in patterns of revolutionary belief, and that institutions and practices were then brought into line with these. Others contend that the Revolution actually represented an intellectual catching-up, a coming to grips with developments that had already taken place in the social and political structure by the mid-eighteenth century. At issue here is the basic question of determining whether rapid and extensive social change is most likely to occur in a society's patterns of thought and belief, practices and behavior, or the formal institutional structure. Here again the reader will want to frame his own answers.

These, then, are some of the basic questions relating to the character and function of revolutionary ideology which the selections in this volume are designed to help understand. It will be evident at once that the essays are by no means in agreement and should be read carefully and critically.

In the first selection Edmund S. Morgan gives some reasons for the political preoccupations of the revolutionary generation. The revolutionary experience, he suggests, completed a basic reorientation of American intellectual life from essentially religious to predominantly political and constitutional themes. Examining changes in the intellectual climate, the internal history of the religious community, and the structure of colonial society as a whole, Morgan asserts that by the middle of the eighteenth century the force of religious arguments and the status of religious leadership had been seriously weakened. This process was considerably accelerated during the revolutionary crisis as political argumentation and constitutional reconstruction became of dominant importance. Concepts of natural rights, government by consent, political equality and representation replaced the doctrine of salvation by grace as the chief foci of intellectual concern. And men who could organize a revolutionary committee or elaborate theories of natural law or parse a constitution succeeded religious exhorters as the primary spokesmen of American society. How valid is Morgan's thesis? He observes that the political ideology of the Revolution revolved around the concept of republicanism. How does he define this term?

Several of the essays discuss the intellectual context of revolutionary ideology. R. A. Humphreys emphasizes the revolutionary generation's dependence upon the legalistic tradition of English constitutional law. The writings of the American Revolution, he affirms, constituted "to an uncommon degree" a legal literature. From first to last, the colonists justified their actions "either on the principles of constitutional or natural law, or of both." This, he points out, led directly to the most significant of all colonial arguments: the notion that every governmental power must be limited by a controlling rule of law. Where does Humphreys find the origin of this colonial attitude? What was its significance for the construction of republican state governments after independence, and for the question of democracy under the new state constitutions?

Caroline Robbins considers another of the intellectual traditions that influenced the republican ideology of the United States: that of the Commonwealthmen, or Real Whigs, of eighteenth-century England. Building upon the writings of John Milton, Algernon Sidney, and James Harrington, political theorists of the English Civil War era (1641–1660), several succeeding generations of pamphleteers fashioned a radical critique of English political life. Existing outside and to the left of the dominant political system, the Commonwealthmen sought to reform prevailing political and constitutional arrangements. Persuaded that the growing strength of the Crown and its ministers threatened to subvert the House of Commons, the only truly representative branch of the government, the Commonwealthmen argued vigorously for an effective separation and balance of powers. Seeking more responsible government, they called for expansion of the suffrage and a redistribution of seats in the Commons more in accord with existing patterns of population. On a more general level, they insisted that men should be ruled only by laws to which they themselves have consented and called for wider freedom of thought and expression. In their lifetimes, Robbins concludes, the Commonwealthmen could claim few tangible achievements within England. They did, however, keep alive an important dissenting tradition and, what is more, transmitted this tradition to America, where it found concrete expression in the constitutional formulations of the revolutionary generation.

In studying the selection, try to determine how radical this dissenting tradition really was in the context of both eighteenth-century England and the American colonies. Aside from their specific proposals (extension of the franchise, etc.), the writings of the Commonwealthmen may have served in two ways the important psychological function of legitimizing America's revolt: by pointing up (from inside English society) the shortcomings of England's political and constitutional order and by linking the colonists with a historic republican tradition traceable to the English Civil War and beyond that to the glorious days of republican Greece and Rome.

Perry Miller introduces the difficult question of determining the significance of religious rhetoric for the revolutionary experience. Building upon his detailed analysis of earlier American Puritanism, he argues that the traditional federal theology, particularly the notion of a mutual covenant, or compact, between God and His specially chosen Anglo-American people, provided Americans with both an explanation of their trials at the hands of England and an imperative for doing revolutionary battle in defense of their own divinely appointed historic role. In sum, Miller finds the impulse for revolutionary action within the dynamics of religious belief.

Take time to follow Miller's argument carefully, to grasp the essential meaning of the covenant relationship he describes. Compare this essay with the one by Morgan. Which do you find more persuasive? Is your answer perhaps colored by your own attitudes concerning the importance of religion in men's lives? Miller raises with particular clarity the problem of measuring the true significance of a society's rhetoric. How can one distinguish ritualized expressions that have little compelling force even for the persons uttering them, from statements that genuinely reflect a society's efforts to find meaning and direction in life?

One of the chief points of controversy among students of revolutionary political thought (and of eighteenth-century American intellectual history generally) has been the relationship between America and the European Enlightenment. Was there anything that can be called an American Enlightenment, and if so how was it dependent upon or different from its European counterpart? These are questions that Peter Gay confronts in the next essay. He concludes that there was indeed an American Enlightenment, that it assumed certain distinctive forms in keeping with America's unique experience, and that it was clearly reflected in the political and constitutional formulations of the Revolutionary Era. What does Gay find as the essential character of the American Enlightenment? Are his conclusions compatible with those of Humphreys and Miller?

The selection by Louis Hartz leads into a group of several essays dealing more directly with the question of the radicalness of revolutionary political thought. Hartz argues that the American colonies, unlike eighteenth-century France, entered their revolution already in possession of a "free society," having experienced no "feudal" past and thus requiring no process of "democratic" reconstruction. The result was a "frame of mind that cannot be found anywhere else in the eighteenth century," one that he describes as uniformly "liberal." How does he define this American liberalism and how does he explain its appearance? Paradoxically, he finds that in the American context liberalism gave the appearance of "outright conservatism," indeed of "traditionalism." What does he mean by this? Finally, what does he believe to have been the significance of the revolutionary experience as opposed to pre-revolutionary colonial development in the formation of American political thought? Is he really writing about the Revolution or about pre-revolutionary America?

The selection by Hartz (together with several of the earlier essays, particularly those of Humphreys and Miller) emphasizes the conservative character of revolutionary ideology and its continuities with earlier patterns of colonial thought. Other scholars have stressed the discontinuities of revolutionary thought, its freshness and originality and its essentially radical character. Moreover they have paid greater attention to the transforming, radicalizing effects that the revolutionary experience had upon American ideas and belief. They maintain that the course of American ideological development took a substantially new direction because of the Revolution. The central focus of this departure is identified with the concept of republicanism. As the reader proceeds, he will want to pay close attention to the ways in which this theme is developed.

As we have already seen, one major concern of students of the Revolution has been to examine its internal history, to judge how much of a struggle between competing classes, sections, or other interest groups accompanied the contest with England and how radical, or democratic, the results of this struggle were. Elisha P. Douglass addresses himself to this point and finds that within the revolutionary movement there were indeed different political philosophies, based upon long-standing divisions in colonial society. These he labels Whig and democratic. The Whig philosophy, he suggests, reflected the beliefs of such revolutionary leaders as John Adams, and had as its goal independence and American self-government, but not internal social or political reform. This was the attitude of men already in positions of political power who wished to carry over into independence established institutions and patterns of leadership. The democratic set of attitudes was held by less privileged members of society—individuals and groups traditionally without political power who believed that the Whig leaders were using the Revolution only to throw off British influence and to establish themselves more firmly in command. Accordingly, these democratic elements set about the task of challenging the Whig leadership to apply the Revolution's precepts at home as well as abroad. Their goal was genuinely democratic reform within the new state governments. Douglass finds that in the end the democratic efforts enjoyed but limited success. The main thrust of the revolutionary experience, he concludes, was eminently conservative.

In reading the selection, consider some of the implications of Douglass' arguments. Does he believe ideology to be simply a form of special pleading, of rationalization for selfish personal or group interests? Compare his arguments on this point with those of the other authors. Finally, is he fully justified in his labeling of the Whig position as conservative? In trying to answer this, pay close attention to his use of the terms "radical" and "democratic."

One way to gain perspective on the radicalness of American revolutionary thought is by comparing it with other revolutionary experiences. R. R. Palmer does this in his *Age of the Democratic Revolution* and finds that during the late eighteenth century Europe and America were swept by a common revolutionary movement powerfully democratic in character. Its effects, he explains, were felt most dramatically in France and America. The result was "a new feeling for a kind of equality . . . a discomfort with older forms of social stratification and social rank." Politically this democratic ferment was directed against control of government by privileged and self-recruiting groups of men. It denied that any person should exercise coercive authority simply by right of his own status or the processes of history, and it emphasized the delegation of authority and the removability of political officials.

It is a central part of Palmer's argument that the American Revolution (like the French) was decidedly democratic in character and that it effected truly democratic reforms. In what specific ways does he claim this to have been true? Is the radicalness of American political ideas to be found in their content or elsewhere? Palmer concludes that the American revolutionary experience was neither fully radical nor strictly conservative; it remained ambivalent. Should one infer from this that efforts to label the Revolution either radical or conservative are oversimplifications?

Gordon S. Wood finds that a radical transformation in American political thought took place during the Revolutionary years. He argues that this involved most fundamentally a rejection of former loyalties to the notion of limited monarchy and a conscious, indeed self-conscious, adoption of republican theories of government and society—a newly affirmed belief that liberty was compatible only with a republican system. Involved in this dramatic shift in American thought, he suggests, was a basic reconstruction of America's self-image, of the ways in which the American people thought about themselves and the kind of ideal future which they projected. Elaborating more fully than any of the other authors upon the content of this republican ideology, Wood emphasizes its inclusiveness. It involved, he observes, a total system of values and beliefs, significantly utopian in character, capable of explaining history and putting man and society into a meaningful perspective. It was, as well, a dynamic ideology, containing profound social implications which called for the re-evaluation of human institutions and the achievement of republican reform.

The reader will certainly want to compare Wood's vivid description of this republican faith with the comments of the preceding authors. Note, for example, that he is dealing with many of the same individuals whom Douglass labels as Whigs, yet he comes away with a quite different reading of their basic beliefs. What are the elements of the republican ideology that Wood describes? Which of these constituted departures from earlier patterns of colonial thought? What kinds of social and political reform did America's newly found republican faith demand?

At the end of his essay, Wood observes that "the revolution the Americans eventually achieved was not precisely the revolution they intended, and it may in fact have been more revolutionary than the original aim." The next selection develops this idea in some detail. More than any other item in this volume, Bernard Bailyn's essay points up the dynamic, self-radicalizing character of the republican ideology. The Revolution, he declares, effected a major transformation

in American political belief. Yet this was only in part the result of conscious design.
The revolutionary generation, he writes, "found a new world of political thought as
they struggled to work out the implications of their beliefs in the years before
independence." Focusing on the theme of political representation, he describes the
transformation of attitudes and belief that resulted from the developing radicalism
of the revolutionary debate. Bailyn finds impressive changes taking place in the
broader mood and temper of political life as well. Under the continuing pressure of
revolutionary upheaval, he argues, the "contagion of liberty" eroded traditional
habits of deference shown by lesser men to their superiors and encouraged the
practice of questioning rather than automatically accepting established authority.

Read the first paragraphs of the Bailyn selection with particular care, for in it
is compressed an important part of the argument, including both Bailyn's assumptions concerning the kinds and amounts of change brought to American society by
the Revolution and his explanation of why the Revolution makes most sense considered as an intellectual movement. What was the specific function of revolutionary ideology as described in these pages? Was it to provide an intellectual catching-
up with changes that a century and a half of life in the New World had already
brought about? Or did ideology serve primarily as a dynamic force for further
change? The reader will need to consider both parts of the argument and relate
them to each other.

The final selection, a second essay by Gordon S. Wood, serves to draw together some of the material so far presented and to clarify one of the major problems
of analysis with which we have been concerned. First, Wood presents a historiographical analysis of the literature dealing with revolutionary political thought.
Secondly, he elaborates upon the two basic approaches to the study of revolutionary political thought—idealist and behaviorist—which scholars have employed
over the years and explains the differences between them concerning their assumptions about the ways men think and the relationship between thought and action.
Each of the two modes of analysis, he finds, has demonstrated certain strengths and
weaknesses, but has alone proved inadequate. The present need, he suggests, is for
a joining together of both idealist and behaviorist approaches, and he makes some
effort to show how this might be done.

One point on which Wood insists is that students of intellectual history must
take into account the unconscious as well as the conscious, the irrational as well as
the rational sources of men's ideas. If true, how is this to be done? Does it require a
different kind of reading of the records with which intellectual history deals? The
historian, he also argues, should be concerned not with justifying a body of thought
but rather with explaining it. Would the authors of this volume agree? Would you?

If the idealist historian conceives of ideas as having a life and logic of their
own apart from any social context, if the behaviorist assumes that ideas have no
reality apart from surrounding social conditions and experience, and if Wood
believes neither of these positions acceptable by itself—what then does he take to

be the "true" relationship between ideology and its social context, between the levels of thought and action in human affairs? How would you answer this? Does the answer perhaps vary for different periods of history, for different types of social situations, for different kinds of ideological systems (for example, systematic philosophy as opposed to patterns of popular belief)?

Hopefully these readings will aid in the search for answers to some of the questions that have been posed—questions that must be carefully considered by anyone attempting to understand the American Revolutionary Era.

In the reprinted selections footnotes appearing in the original sources have in general been omitted unless they contribute to the argument or better understanding of the selection.

Historians frequently note that the Revolution represented a watershed in America's intellectual as well as social and political development. By this they mean that with the Revolution the change from an essentially religious to a primarily secular and political cultural orientation was completed. In the Revolutionary Era, America's distinguishing problems were no longer religious organization or the salvation of men's souls but constitutional reconstruction, economic development, and geographical expansion—secular and political issues all of them. EDMUND S. MORGAN (b. 1916), Sterling Professor of American History at Yale, describes the historical background of this development. Among his writings are *The Puritan Family* (1944), *The Stamp Act Crisis* (1953), and *Visible Saints* (1963).*

Edmund S. Morgan

The Revolutionary Era as an Age of Politics

In 1740 America's leading intellectuals were clergymen and thought about theology; in 1790 they were statesmen and thought about politics. A variety of forces, some of them reaching deep into the colonial past, helped to bring about the transformation, but it was so closely associated with the revolt from England that one may properly consider the American Revolution, as an intellectual movement, to mean the substitution of political for clerical leadership and of politics for religion as the most challenging area of human thought and endeavor.

The American colonies had been founded during the seventeenth century, when Englishmen were still animated by the great vision of John Calvin, the vision

of human depravity and divine perfection. Every human being from Adam onward must be counted, Calvin insisted, in the ranks of "those whose feet are swift to shed blood, whose hands are polluted with rapine and murder, whose throats are like open sepulchres, whose tongues are deceitful, whose lips are envenomed, whose works are useless, iniquitous, corrupt, and deadly, whose souls are estranged from God, the inmost recesses of whose hearts are full of pravity, whose eyes are insidiously employed, whose minds are elated with insolence—in a word, all whose powers are prepared for the commission of atrocious and innumerable crimes." If a man did not actually commit such crimes, it was not for want of a desire to. God might fur-

*From Edmund S. Morgan, "The American Revolution Considered as an Intellectual Movement" in Arthur M. Schlesinger, Jr. and Morton M. White (eds.), *Paths of American Thought.* Copyright © 1963 by Houghton Mifflin Company. Reprinted by permission of the publisher. Pp. 11–26. Footnotes omitted.

nish restraints of one sort or another to prevent "the perverseness of our nature from breaking out into external acts, but does not purify it within."

The official church of England, born of a licentious monarch's divorce, had never fully shared in Calvin's vision. Though it absorbed much of his theology during the reign of Queen Elizabeth I, it retained a more flattering view than his of human capacities and priestly powers. The more thoroughgoing English Calvinists, the Puritans, were hopeful of effecting further reforms, but during the late 1620's and 1630's the Church and the king who headed it drew ever closer to old Roman Catholic doctrines. In the 1640's the Puritans resorted to arms, killed the king, purged the Church, and turned England into a republic. But in 1660 the monarchy was restored. Puritans, now called dissenters, were dismissed from office in both church and state; and the Church of England resumed its old ways, unimpeded by Calvinism.

It is no coincidence that England's American colonies were settled before 1640 or after 1660. Emigration offered a substitute for revolution to thousands of men and women who were discontented with the Church of England and with the government that fostered it. Puritans settled all the New England colonies, overran the Catholic refuge of the Calvert family in Maryland, and later furnished substantial numbers of settlers to New York, New Jersey, and the Carolinas. They came even to Virginia, where the majority of settlers, though remaining within the Church of England, did not share in its high-church movement. After the Restoration, the colonies attracted large numbers of English Quakers and Scotch-Irish Presbyterians, not to mention French Huguenots and German Protestants of various denominations. Anglicans came too, and the Angli-

can Church was supported by law in several colonies, but the flavor of American colonial life was overwhelmingly that of the Reformation.

The intellectual center of the colonies was New England, and the intellectual leaders of New England were the clergy, who preached and wrote indefatigably of human depravity and divine perfection. These two axioms, for the Puritans as for Calvin himself, required the eternal damnation of most of mankind. And since God knew all and decreed all from eternity, it followed that He had determined in advance who should be damned and who should be saved. One of the principal tasks of the ministry was to explain to men how bad they were, so bad that they all deserved damnation. That God had chosen to save any was simply through mercy, another attribute of His perfection. No man deserved salvation, no one was less guilty than another, so that God's choice rested only in Himself.

To explain these doctrines was the easiest part of the preacher's task, for most of his audience were already persuaded of them. A more difficult assignment was to assist men in discerning where they stood in the divine scheme. No man could be certain whether he was saved until the day of judgment, but there were stages in the process of redemption that took place in this life; and ministers devoted much of their preaching and writing to descriptions of them. . . .

Just as the Puritans' theology revolved around human depravity and divine perfection, so did their political theory. And Puritan ministers instructed their congregations in politics as well as religion. They taught that society originates in a contract between God on the one hand and the people on the other, whereby if the people agreed to abide by His commands (though again, only outwardly, for true, inner obedience was beyond them) He would assure them outward prosperity. Having made such an agreement, the people, in another compact, voluntarily subjected themselves to a king or to other civil rulers. This was the origin of government; and the purpose of government was to restrain the sinfulness of man, to prevent and punish offenses against God. As long as a king enforced God's commands, embodying them in human laws, the people owed him obedience and assistance. If, however, moved by his own depravity, he violated God's commands or failed to enforce them, he broke the compact on which his political authority rested, and it was the people's duty to remove him lest God visit the whole community with death and destruction.

These ideas had developed in England at a time when reigning monarchs exhibited (by Puritan standards) far too much depravity. Three generations of Puritans nervously scolded their kings and queens and momentarily expected God's wrath to descend on England. Finally, in 1649, they did away with both king and kingship. But even after monarchy ended, human depravity remained, and Englishmen faced the problem of controlling it in the new context of a republic. Ideas about the maintenance of purity, probity, and stability in a republic were offered by a number of men, the most influential of whom was James Harrington. In his *Oceana* (1656) Harrington associated republican government with widespread distribution—approaching equality—of property. He also advocated religious toleration, rotation in public office, and separation of governmental powers. With the restoration of the monarchy, Harrington's work continued for several generations to excite the admiration of a small group of British political thinkers, who probed the nature of government and speculated about methods of keeping it responsible to the people. The best known of them, John Locke, reemphasized the idea of a compact between rulers and people in order to justify the exclusion of James II from the throne.

The English republican writers were read in the colonies, and Locke's political doctrines were assimilated by American clergymen and dispensed in their sermons along with the older ideas. Every generation learned of its duty to pull down bad rulers and to uphold good ones. The colonists did not, however, develop a separate school of republican political theory. The clergy, who continued to be the principal exponents of political ideas and the most influential members of the community, devoted their creative intellectual efforts to theology, and their congregations continued to search souls. Every Sunday they attended at the meetinghouse morning and afternoon to hear the theological expositions that were always the principal ingredient in a Puritan church service. Then they went home to write in their diaries and measure their lives against what they had learned in the sermons. Daily they read their Bibles and prayed in private and with their families. Theology was as much a part of their lives as meat and drink.

By the middle of the eighteenth century, however, a change had begun. A series of developments, culminating in the Revolution, combined to effect a weakening of popular interest in theology and a decline in clerical leadership.

The first development, and the most difficult to assess, was the growth in England and Europe, transmitted gradually to America, of a new confidence in human reason. The achievements of Sir Isaac Newton and of other seventeenth-century astronomers and mathematicians belied the low estimate hitherto entertained of man's capacity to understand, without the assistance of divine revelation, God's government of the universe. The Enlightenment, as the new attitude came to be called, promised to reveal the mysteries of creation simply through the application of human intelligence.

New England ministers at first perceived no threat to religion from the Enlightenment. Although they thought poorly of human reason, they were themselves assiduous in making the most of it. They had applied it primarily to the Bible, but they now welcomed every new piece of observational knowledge in the assurance that it would help to fill out the data derived from the Bible. With the success of Newton to spur them, they began to pay more attention to the physical world and made observations of plants and animals, of comets and stars; and they sent these observations to England to assist the progress of knowledge about God's wonderful universe.

It became apparent only gradually—first in England, then in America—that reason, instead of assisting revelation, might replace it. Though Newton himself retained a firm belief in the Scriptures and spent his later years unraveling Biblical prophecies, many of his admirers became deists, who believed that God reveals Himself only through the operation of His universe and not through prophets, priests, or holy scriptures. In America deism claimed few adherents before the last quarter of the eighteenth century; and it seems probable that the Enlightenment appreciably lowered the prestige of the clergy only after they had already lost much of their influence through the paradoxical operation of a religious revival.

The Great Awakening of the 1740s began when a young English minister, George Whitefield, showed American preachers how to convey the full meaning of human depravity. Traveling throughout the colonies, he preached wherever he could find an audience, whether inside a church or under a tree, and everywhere his message was the same: men deserve hell.

Whitefield's talent lay in depicting the torments of hell dramatically and vividly. He could weep at will, over the fate of the men and women before him; he could impersonate God delivering the awful sentence against them. When he wept they did too, and when he pronounced the sentence against them, they fell to the ground in agony.

Whitefield had already earned some notoriety by these methods before crossing the ocean. In the colonies his success was overwhelming. People flocked to him as to a new messiah. Though Anglicans remained largely unmoved, most Americans had been brought up on the doctrine of the depravity of man, and they could not find any expression of it too strong. Whitefield merely brought them a new and more emotional appreciation of truths they had known all along. Other preachers quickly imitated his methods and outdid him in the extravagance of their gestures. Gilbert Tennent of Pennsylvania made a specialty of roaring with holy laughter at sinners whom he had awakened to their helpless condition. James Davenport of Long Island liked to preach at night, when smoking candles and torches gave verisimilitude to his fiery denunciations. These self-appointed apostles and dozens more like them imitated Whitefield not only in their manner of preaching but in wandering from place to place to deliver their fearful message.

Terror was the object; and terror was right. If a man faces eternal, unbearable pain, deserves it, and can do nothing to avoid it, he ought to be terrified. The preachers had another word for it, familiar to all Calvinists: they called it conviction, the awareness, denied to the complacent, of one's hopeless condition. The great thing about the new preaching was that it destroyed complacency and brought conviction to thousands. And the great thing about conviction was that conversion could be expected in many cases to follow it. Calvinist ministers for two centuries had described the divine process, and in the Great Awakening the course of conviction and conversion ran true to form. Not everyone who trembled in terror rose to the joy of conversion, but hundreds did.

As the churches filled with them, it seemed apparent that God approved the new method of preaching and the men who practiced it. Whether He also approved the older methods was questionable. Men and women who had worshiped for years without result under the guidance of an erudite but undramatic minister, found grace after a few hours at the feet of some wandering apostle. The itinerant was often a layman who had never been to college and knew no Greek, Latin, or Hebrew, but had a way with an audience. If God selected him to do so much without learning, was learning perhaps more a hindrance than a help to true religion? The thought occurred to many converts and was encouraged by the increasingly confident, not to say arrogant, posture of the itinerants. Whitefield had warned broadly against ministers who preached an unknown and unfelt Christ. His followers did not hesitate to name individual ministers as dead of heart, blind leaders of the blind.

After such a pronouncement, a congregation, or a substantial portion of it, might desert their old minister. If they were a majority, they could dismiss him; if a minority, they might secede to form a church of their own, with some newly discovered prophet to lead them. Congregations had left their ministers before, especially in New England, but never before had the desertions been so many or so bitter.

At first the deserted clergymen merely looked upon the Awakening with skepticism. But as its exponents (known to the time as New Lights) became more and more extravagant, skepticism spread and grew to hostility. Ministers who had spent their lives in the study of theology and who had perhaps been touched by the Enlightenment, were appalled at the ignorance of New Light preachers and dismissed their convictions and conversions as hysteria. ... The majority, clinging to the old doctrines of Calvinism, mitigated in some measure by the Enlightenment, were a humane and pious group, perhaps the most likeable of New England clergymen. Some of them retained or rewon the loyalty of large congregations. But they never regained the broad influence they had enjoyed over the colonial community before the Great Awakening.

The failure of the Old Light clergy to retain intellectual leadership was partly to the fact that they failed to win the minds of the next generation of ministers. The New Lights, in spite of their ignorance, enjoyed the blessing of Jonathan Edwards, America's foremost intellectual. It was inevitable that bright young divinity students should follow his lead. Edwards, the most brilliant theologian the country ever produced, had already generated a minor awakening of his own at Northampton, Massachusetts, six years before the Great Awakening. By comparison with Whitefield his technique was muted: he talked almost in a monotone, and never resorted to dramatic gestures, but when he spoke of eternal torments in as matter-of-fact a manner as he spoke of the weather, the effect on a New England audience could be devastating. Observing the beneficial effects of terror, Edwards applauded when Whitefield and Tennent brought the fires of hell to New England.

In ensuing years Edwards wrote a series of treatises to demonstrate the importance of the emotions or "affections" in religion and to affirm, more rigorously than ever before in New England, the dogmas of divine perfection and human depravity. By the time he died in 1758, he had gathered a tight band of followers, who continued his doctrines and developed them into a theological system known as the New Divinity. The high priest of the movement was Samuel Hopkins, who preached at Great Barrington, Massachusetts, and later at Newport, Rhode Island. Other leading figures were Edwards's son, Jonathan Jr., of New Haven, and Joseph Bellamy, who from the small village of Bethlehem, Connecticut, earned the title of pope of Litchfield County.

New Divinity men were often rough and domineering with their congregations, exploding in angry denunciations; and their doctrines matched their manners. It was wrong, they said, for the unregenerate to pray, since an unregenerate man, lacking real love for God, could not pray without hypocrisy and would anger God further by his futile efforts. The only way in which the unregenerate could contribute to the glory of God was to rejoice in their own damnation—an attitude which their very unregeneracy made improbable. The New Divinity also called for a restoration of the standards of church membership that had prevailed in New England before the Half-Way Covenant of 1662: a man could join the church only if he demonstrated to the satisfaction of the other members that God had predestined him to eternal salvation. Only such persons were entitled to take communion or to have their children baptized. The remainder of the community could only listen to the minister's preaching in hopes that God would use this means to achieve a salvation already determined though as yet undisclosed.

The New Divinity had a consistency and rigor that young intellectuals found challenging. It was the fashionable, avant-garde movement of the seventeen-fifties, sixties, seventies, and to some extent the eighties. During these years many young men had already begun to find politics or the law more satisfying intellectually than religion, but insofar as religion continued to draw young minds, they gravitated to men like Bellamy and Hopkins for guidance. As a result, by 1792 the New Divinity claimed half the pulpits in Connecticut (and an increasing number in the rest of New England), together with virtually all the candidates for the ministry—this on the testimony of Ezra Stiles, president of Yale from 1778 to 1795, who despised the New Divinity and lamented its attraction for the young men he had educated.

But the success of the New Divinity among the rising generation of clergy was not matched among the people at large. Its harsh doctrines could be sustained only by intellectual or religious fervor, and the religious fervor of Americans was already waning before the complexities of the system had been completely worked out. Even as Jonathan Edwards turned out his massive justifications of the Great Awakening, that movement subsided in the manner of later religious revivals. By the time Edwards had devised an intellectual foundation for emotionalism in religion, he had begun to lose his popular audience. When he announced that he would apply new standards of church membership, excluding all but the demonstrably regenerate from the sacraments, his church at Northampton dismissed him. America's greatest intellectual of his time spent most of his later years preaching, for want of a wider audience, to the Indians, who perhaps least of any group in America could understand him. . . .

[The New Divinity clergys'] fault lay in addressing themselves more to each other than to their people. Engrossed in the details of their system, they delighted in exploring new elements of consistency in it and neglected the central problems of

Christianity, until they scarcely knew how to deal with the elementary questions of salvation that their people put to them. . . .

The clergy for the first time in their history had lost contact with the people. In the seventeenth century when Roger Williams debated fine points of theology with John Cotton, or Increase Mather with Solomon Stoddard, people had not been bored. But the New Divinity ministers were unable to carry their congregations with them.

In earlier decades when a people became disgruntled with their minister, they had replaced him. But the American population had increased so rapidly that there were not enough ministers to go around; and since the New Divinity claimed such a large percentage of ministerial candidates, congregations were regularly faced with the necessity of taking a New Divinity man or leaving their pulpit vacant. The resultant discontent contributed in the last quarter of the eighteenth century to the rapid growth of Anglicanism, Methodism, deism, and what people at the time called "nothingarianism," a total indifference to religion. The clergy, once the most respected members of the community, became the objects of ridicule and contempt, especially in Connecticut, the stronghold of the New Divinity. In 1788, when the ministers of the state published a rebuke to the people for their neglect of public worship, the newspapers carried some rude answers. "We have heard your animadversions," said one, "upon our absence from Sabbath meetings, and humbly conceive if you wish our attendance there, you would make it worth our while to give it. To miss a sermon of the present growth, what is it but to miss of an opiate? And can the loss of a nap expose our souls to eternal perdition?"

Such indifference to religion, edged with hostility to the clergy, was the end product of the developments we have been tracing from the 1740's. But though the clergy could blame themselves for much of their loss of prestige and for much of the decline of popular interest in religion, it was Parliament's attempt to tax the colonists in the 1760's that caused Americans to transfer to politics the intellectual interest and energy that were once reserved for religion. This reorientation was directed partly by the clergy themselves. They had never stopped giving instruction in political thought; and (except for the Anglicans) throughout the 1760s and 1770s they publicly and passionately scored the actions of George III and his Parliament against the standards by which their English Puritan predecessors had judged and condemned Charles I.

Presbyterian and Congregational ministers also raised the alarm when a movement was set afoot for the establishment in the colonies of state-supported bishops. The American clergymen developed no new general ideas about government—there was no New Light in political thought, no New Politics to match the New Divinity—but the old ideas and those imported from English political theorists served well enough to impress upon their congregations the tyrannical nature of taxation without representation, and of bishops who might establish ecclesiastical courts with jurisdiction extending beyond their own denomination.

Although the clergy were a powerful influence in molding American political opinion during the Revolutionary period, they did not recover through politics the intellectual leadership they had already begun to lose. Their own principles barred them from an active role in politics. While they had always given political advice freely and exercised their influence in elections, most of them would have considered it wrong to sit in a representative assembly, on a governor's council, or on the bench.

To them as to their Puritan ancestors the clerical exercise of temporal powers spelled Rome. A minister's business was, after all, the saving of souls. By the same token, however outraged he might be by the actions of the English government, however excited by the achievement of American independence, a minister could not devote his principal intellectual effort to the expounding of political ideas and political principles. As the quarrel with England developed and turned into a struggle for independence and nationhood, though the ministers continued to speak up on the American side, other voices commanding greater attention were raised by men who were free to make a career of politics and prepared to act as well as talk.

There had always, of course, been political leaders in the colonies, but hitherto politics had been a local affair, requiring at most the kind of talents needed for collecting votes or pulling wires. A colonial legislative assembly might occasionally engage in debates about paper money, defense, or modes of taxation; but the issues did not reach beyond the borders of the colony involved and were seldom of a kind to challenge a superior mind. No American debated imperial policy in the British Parliament, the Privy Council, or the Board of Trade. The highest political post to which a man could aspire in the colonies was that of governor, and everywhere except in Connecticut and Rhode Island, this was obtained not through political success but through having friends in England. Few native Americans ever achieved it or even tried to.

But the advent of Parliamentary taxation inaugurated a quarter-century of political discussion in America that has never since been matched in intensity. With the passage of the Stamp Act in 1765, every colonial legislature took up the task of defining the structure of the British empire;

and as colonial definitions met with resistance from England, as the colonies banded together for defense and declared their independence, politics posed continental, even global, problems that called forth the best efforts of the best American minds. In no other period of our history would it be possible to find in politics five men of such intellectual stature as Benjamin Franklin, John Adams, Alexander Hamilton, James Madison, and Thomas Jefferson; and there were others only slightly less distinguished.

Whether they hailed from Pennsylvania or Virginia, New England or New York, the men who steered Americans through the Revolution, the establishment of a new nation, and the framing of the Constitution did not for the most part repudiate the political ideas inherited from the period of clerical dominance. Like the clergy, they started from a conviction of human depravity; like the clergy, they saw government originating in compact, and measured governmental performance against an absolute standard ordained by God. Like the clergy too, they found inspiration in the example of seventeenth-century Englishmen. . . .

Indeed, most of the ideas about government which American intellectuals employed first in their resistance to Parliament, and then in constructing their own governments, had been articulated earlier in England and were still in limited circulation there. The social compact, fundamental law, the separation of powers, human equality, religious freedom, and the superiority of republican government were continuing ideals for a small but ardent group of Englishmen who, like the Americans, believed that the British constitution was basically republican and drew inspiration from it while attacking the ministers and monarch who seemed to be betraying it. It is perhaps no accident that the work in which Americans first repudiated monarchy, *Common Sense,* was written by an Englishman, Thomas Paine, who had come to America only two years before.

But if Englishmen supplied the intellectual foundations both for the overthrow of English rule and for the construction of republican government, Americans put the ideas into practice and drew on American experience and tradition to devise refinements and applications of the greatest importance. That republican ideas, which existed in a state of obscurity in England, should be congenial in the colonies, was due in the first place to the strong continuing Calvinist tradition which had been nourished over the years by the American clergy. But fully as important was the fact that during a hundred and fifty years of living in the freedom of a relatively isolated and empty continent, the colonists had developed a way of life in which republican ideas played a visible part. When Parliamentary taxation set Americans to analyzing their relationship to the mother country, they could not escape seeing that the social, economic and political configuration of America had diverged from that of England in ways that made Americans better off than Englishmen. And the things that made them better off could be labeled republican.

England's practical experience with republicanism had lasted only eleven years. With the return of Charles II in 1660, Englishmen repudiated their republic and the Puritans who had sponsored it. Though a small minority continued to write and talk about republicanism and responsible government, they wielded no authority. The House of Commons grew more powerful but less common, and the main current of English national life flowed in the channels of monarchy, aristocracy, and special privilege. Americans, by contrast, though formally subjects of the

king, had lived long under conditions that approximated the ideals of the English republican theorists. Harrington thought he had found in the England of his day the widespread ownership of property that seemed to him a necessary condition for republican government; but thoughout the colonies ownership of property had always been more widespread than in England. Furthermore no member of the nobility had settled in America, so that people were accustomed to a greater degree of social as well as economic equality than existed anywhere in England. . . .

Though the English people had twice removed an unsatisfactory king, in 1649 and in 1688, the English government remained far less responsible and far less responsive to the people than any colonial government. While the members of Parliament disclaimed any obligation to their immediate constituents, the members of American representative assemblies knew that they were expected to look after the interests of the people who elected them. Nor were the voters in America only a small minority of the population as in England. In most colonies probably the great majority of adult males owned enough property to meet the qualification (which varied from colony to colony) for voting. In England, the government paid hundreds of office-holders whose offices, carrying no duties, existed solely for the enrichment of those who held them. In the colonies such sinecures were few. Americans thought that government existed to do a job, and they created no offices except for useful purposes.

Thus when the quarrel with Parliament began, the colonists already had what English reformers wanted. And the colonists were inclined to credit their good fortune not to the accident of geography but to their own superior virtue and political sophistication. The interpretation was not

without foundation: since Calvinist traditions were still strong among them and
since they had often learned of British republican ideas through the sermons of Calvinist clergymen, Americans retained what
the Enlightenment had dimmed in England and Europe, a keen sense of human
depravity and of the dangers it posed for
government. Although their own governments had hitherto given little evidence of
depravity, by comparison with those of Europe, they were expert at detecting it in
any degree. They had always been hor-
rified by the open corruption of British politics and feared it would lead to tyranny.
When Parliament attempted to tax them
and sent swarms of customs collectors, sail-
ors, and soldiers to support the attempt,
their fears were confirmed. In resisting the
British and in forming their own governments, they saw the central problem as one
of devising means to check the inevitable
operation of depravity in men who wielded
power. English statesmen had succumbed
to it. How could Americans avoid their
mistakes?

In the era of the American Revolution,
from 1764 to 1789, this was the great intellectual challenge. Although human depravity continued to pose as difficult theological problems as ever, the best minds of the
period addressed themselves to the rescue
not of souls, but of governments, from the
perils of corruption. . . .

Of the intellectual currents feeding into American revolutionary political thought, none were more important than the traditions of English common and constitutional law. Many of the central problems of the revolutionary years were essentially constitutional in nature; namely, the proper distribution of authority within the empire (among Crown, Parliament, and the colonial legislatures) and the internal structure of the new state and continental governments. In the following article, R. A. HUMPHREYS (b. 1907), a specialist in both the revolutionary and national periods of Latin American history, discusses the legal and constitutional aspects of American revolutionary thought. Some people would argue that constitutional issues become important only when activated by more basic political, social, or economic conflicts. Do you agree? Does Humphreys take this argument adequately into account?*

R. A. Humphreys

The Rule of Law and
the American Revolution

The American colonies of the seventeenth century were dependent communities legally subject to the authority of the English Crown. The history of their constitutional development in the first half of the eighteenth century is essentially the history of the efforts of the colonial assemblies to establish their supremacy within the colonies and over the instruments of the royal prerogative. In their conflicts with the Crown and its agents the colonies won repeated victories; and from Parliament they had received support rather than opposition. To what extent they were themselves subject to the authority of Parliament was a question which had only indirectly arisen, and which, so long as that authority was exerted only in matters of general and external polity, troubled them little. But while the revolution settlement had defined in some important respects the limits of the royal prerogative—in itself a notable assertion of parliamentary supremacy—the two Houses of Parliament had continually strengthened their control over the executive authority of the Crown. They had displayed increasing interest and activity in the affairs of the colonies. Above all, they had asserted more and more confidently that there was, in Lord Mansfield's words, "no restriction to the legislative authority of Great Britain." It thus followed that in the moment of their victory over the instruments of the royal

*From R. A. Humphreys, "The Rule of Law and the American Revolution," *Law Quarterly Review* (1937), 80–98. Footnotes omitted.

prerogative, the colonial assemblies found themselves threatened by the omnipotent claims of a distant legislature. . . .

By the middle of the eighteenth century, then, not only had the two Houses [of Parliament] greatly extended their control over the executive authority of the Crown, but the doctrine of the absolute legal sovereignty of the Crown in Parliament had been firmly established. . . . "Let us avow . . . ", wrote Bentham in 1776, "steadily but calmly . . . that the authority of the supreme body [i.e., Parliament] cannot, *unless where limited by express convention,* be said to have any assignable, any certain bounds. That to say there is any act they *cannot* do—to speak of any thing of their's as being *illegal*—as being *void;*—to speak of their exceeding their *authority* (whatever be the phrase)—their *power,* their *right*—is, however common, an abuse of language.". . .

Between the two Houses of Parliament thus wielding the weapon of omnipotence and omnicompetence, and the colonial assemblies lately victorious over the royal prerogative, conflict was bound to occur. For it was precisely this omnipotence and omnicompetence, which they resented in Parliament, that the assemblies had been increasingly prone to arrogate to themselves. They had long striven for parliamentary powers as well as parliamentary forms. They had sought to free themselves from the shackles of royal instructions and judicial review, and to establish their superiority over the colonial executive and the colonial judiciary. They had proved themselves increasingly intolerant of restraints upon their legislative will either within or without the colonies. . . .

The American revolution . . . was carried through on the most conservative principles. The literature of the revolution is eminently a conservative literature, and to an uncommon degree a legal literature.

From beginning to end the justification of the revolution is a legal justification. Combating the novel claims of parliamentary absolutism the colonists based their case either on the principles of constitutional or of natural law, or of both. They appealed first to colonial charters, then to the rights of Englishmen and the nature of the English constitution; finally they cast off their rights as Englishmen to appeal to their rights as men; they turned from the nature of the constitution to nature's laws themselves. And an appeal to the laws of nature and of nature's God was no mere rhetorical flourish. It was an appeal to the most sacred and fundamental of all laws.

These phrases and these appeals might, it is true, have no more than a verbal significance, and represent no more than a conventional usage of words hallowed by tradition and familiar through constant use. The law of nature, for example, implied very different degrees of obligation to Blackstone and to James Otis. What John Adams meant by the sovereignty of the people was something rather different from what Samuel Adams meant. . . . All these phrases, these appeals to precedents and principles, must be construed according to the different directions in which men's minds were intended. They could be invoked for widely different reasons, and their implications might be widely apart. "You know," said Samuel Adams, "there is a charm in the word 'constitutional.' "

But yet this atmosphere of legality is characteristic of the colonial climate of opinion. And it points the way to what was after all the most significant and interesting of the colonial arguments. Parliamentary authority might be rejected because it was competitive, or because it was unpopular. But it was to absolutism as such that many of the colonists passionately objected. They were compelled ultimately to deny the legal authority of Parliament only because Parliament itself denied that its authority was limited by a controlling rule of law. But in rejecting parliamentary absolutism they had no desire to erect the despotism of the people. They had no desire to exchange one absolutism for another. This claim to absolute power, John Quincy Adams maintained in 1831, was precisely the cause of the revolution. "The pretence of an absolute, irresistible, despotic power [existing] in every government *somewhere*," he declared, was "incompatible with the first principle of natural right." Adams was the heir to a great tradition. To the claims of parliamentary omnipotence and omnicompetence the colonists replied that Parliament itself was subject to a rule of law; to absolutism, of whatever predicated, whether of Parliament or people, they could oppose not only charters and constitutional rights, but what was the very foundation of those rights, the fundamental law of God and nature, of which Locke had said that it was "an eternal rule to all men, legislators as well as others," and of which even Blackstone had felt constrained to say, "no human laws are of any validity, if contrary to this."

What did this law of nature mean? How was it discovered? "He who bids the law rule, may be deemed to bid God and Reason alone rule," said Aristotle; and from Aristotle to the eighteenth century the theory of the natural, or ideal law of human society continued to attract the thoughts of men. That the universe was a universe of law, devised by a divine architect, that merely by the use of his "natural faculties" man could bring his life, his morals and his institutions into harmony with this natural and rational order, these were commonplaces of much of eighteenth century thought. To the eighteenth century *philosophes* it was evident that merely by inspecting the nature of the universe around him and nature's voice within him,

man could discover those laws of nature and nature's God which were the only valid laws of politics and morals. This may well be so, and it cannot be denied that the *philosophes* belonged to all countries, and that their writings were well enough known in America. Jefferson, no less than Diderot, was a *philosophe*. But if these doctrines contributed to the colonial climate of opinion, it was because the minds of the colonists were already predisposed to accept them. Theology, history, tradition, all alike confirmed them in their beliefs that men had natural rights, founded on the laws of God and nature, that to preserve these rights governments by compact and consent had been instituted amongst men, and that the eternal laws of nature, discoverable by human reason, were universally valid. It was the traditions of the political and ecclesiastical doctrines of England in the seventeenth century, perhaps refined by the rationalistic atmosphere of the eighteenth century, which survived in the colonies—the traditions of the [English] Civil War and Revolution [of 1688], and the tenets of Puritan theology, kept strong and vigorous by the teaching of the New England clergy.

For the Puritan, like the philosopher, saw the universe as a universe of law. If political philosophers spoke of compacts, the Puritan spoke of covenants. They too believed in natural rights protected by unchallengeable law. They too affirmed the existence of a rational order of society, of a universe, indeed, governed according to the strictest legal principles. "God proceeds legally," said John Donne, the Anglican; and the Puritans saw that God had agreed with man in a covenant way: he himself was bound by his own laws. King of kings and lord of lords, he was yet "a constitutional monarch." "The Divine Government," they declared, was "managed by fixed and steady rules." "God himself" said that eminent New England divine, Jonathan Mayhew, "does not govern in an absolutely arbitrary and despotic manner. The power of this Almighty King (I speak it not without caution and reverence); the power of this Almighty King is *limited by law*; not indeed, *by Acts of Parliament,* but by the eternal *laws* of truth, wisdom and equity; and the everlasting *tables* of right reason." The laws of God, then, were the eternal rules of right and reason; they were the natural and rational laws of human society; and they were revealed not merely in the universe around us. They were planted deep in the minds of men, and they were written for all to read in Holy Writ. The law of nature, that part of divine law fathomable by human reason, as reason searched the heart and the scriptures, was an absolute law. No human law was of any validity if contrary to this.

Philosophy and theology alike, then, conducted the colonists to beliefs which they could only regard as self-evident truths. If the Divine Government was managed by fixed and steady rules, so much the more was human authority limited by known and established laws. If God himself was bound by His own laws, so much the more were earthly powers confined by their obligations. If the laws of nature and of nature's God were supreme, all other laws were declaratory, all other authority was partial. Governments existed to preserve those rights which God and nature had given to all, not to reduce them. ("No rational creature," observed Locke, of the contract on which society was based, "can be supposed to change his condition with an intention to be worse.") The very definition of liberty was freedom from arbitrary rule. By compact, charter and consent human authority had been marked out. It followed, therefore, that any act which transcended these limitations was null and void. . . .

What reason and religion taught, history and experience supported. Colonial history, from the beginnings, was compact of charters and covenants in matters both civil and ecclesiastical; and at every turn the colonists were confronted with the spectacle of authority limited by law and agreement. Their own constitutions were "fixed" either in colonial charters or, with some degree of permanence, in the commission and instructions of a governor. The legal spheres of royal and popular authority in the colonies were carefully separated and defined. Such Acts as colonial legislatures passed in excess of their powers were disallowed by the Privy Council in England. And when the colonists thought historically, they did not merely think in terms of Mayflower compacts, charters and covenants, but they thought of the great constitutional struggles of the seventeenth century, of the arguments which common lawyers used against prerogative, of the ideas for which their ancestors suffered, of the Great Rebellion and the Glorious Revolution, of Milton, and of Locke. History, indeed, became philosophy teaching by examples. Aristotle, Cicero, Vattel, what Jefferson called the "elementary books of public right"—and there were many of them—these were familiar enough to the colonists. But it was English ideas and English history of the seventeenth century which they particularly cherished. Had not Harrington pleaded for an empire of laws not of men? Had not Locke declared that the law of nature was an eternal rule to all men, legislators as well as others? . . . There was nothing novel in the colonial belief in a controlling rule of law—though opinions about the nature of that law might differ. . . . " 'Tis hoped," wrote James Otis, "that it will not be considered as a new doctrine, that even the authority of the parliament of *Great-Britain* is circumscribed by certain bounds, which if exceeded their acts become those of meer *power* without *right,* and consequently void. The judges of England have declared in favour of these sentiments, which they expresly declare; that *acts of parliament against natural equity are void.* That *acts against the fundamental principles of the British constitution are void.* This doctrine is agreable to the law of nature and nations, and to the divine dictates of natural and revealed religion."

This passage admirably sums up both the character and the sources of the colonial belief in a controlling rule of law. . . .

It is important to notice the partial identification of this law of nature with the British constitution. Reasonably enough, the colonists assumed that the teachings of this law would be reflected in the experience of man in society, that its light illumined the English common law, that in it the British constitution was founded, a constitution which was not only by far "the best, now existing on earth," but "the best that ever existed among men." "It is the glory of the British constitution," declared the Assembly of Massachusetts Bay, "that it hath its foundations in the law·of God and Nature." But if the constitution was founded in the laws of God and nature, it was therefore rigid as those laws themselves. "In all free states," remarked the assembly, generalizing from its own experience, "the constitution is fixed." Further, "The supreme legislative, in every free state," it affirmed, "derives its power from the constitution; by the fundamental rules of which it is bounded and circumscribed." These rules ascertained and limited both sovereignty and obedience. And the assembly implied that there were certain essential rights so firmly founded "in the law of God and Nature" that in fact they were beyond the reach of parliamentary statute. "To say the parliament is absolute and arbitrary, is a contradiction," declared Otis in a famous passage. "The parliament cannot make 2 and 2, 5; omnipotency cannot do it. The supreme power in a state, is *ius dicere* only;—*ius dare,* strictly speaking, belongs alone to God." An Act contrary to the constitution, contrary to the law of nature, ran his argument, was void; and it was the duty of the Courts to declare it so. But, said Blackstone, no Court may defeat the intent of the Legislature. There is revealed the measure of the difference between the colonial and English interpretations of the constitution.

The colonists, then, assumed that the law of nature was engrafted into the British constitution. The constitution contained a body of fundamental principles; it guaranteed a number of natural rights which no authority within the state could abrogate. But what if, despite the constitution, despite basic common law, what if there should be a difference of opinion about these rights, for they were nowhere very precisely stated? What if Parliament should refuse to admit that its legislative will was subject to a higher law? In that case it might prove impracticable for men who held such contradictory ideas of right to live together in the same society. But this was a conclusion from which the colonists shrunk. And since all their petition was for the laws of England, it seemed, indeed, a monstrous conclusion. . . .

Only reluctantly did the colonists come to the conclusion that it was hopeless to contend that there were limits to parliamentary authority, and that therefore they must deny all parliamentary authority. It was at this point that the American revolution, properly speaking, began. "Whatever difficulty may occur in tracing the line," wrote John Dickinson as late as 1774, "yet we contend, that by the laws of God, and by the laws of the constitution, a line there must be" beyond which parliamentary authority "cannot extend." Dickinson and others had long laboured hard to establish that line by distinguishing between those powers which were proper to parliamentary authority and those which were not. But in vain. "A new party," he complained, had arisen in England, which sought to "erect a new sovereignty over the colonies inconsistent with liberty or freedom." That "new sovereignty," later to receive its systematic definition at the hands of Austin, was consistently attacked by the colonists in the belief that sovereignty was not absolute or arbitrary, but limited and divided. Constitutional and juridical theory failing them, they were compelled ultimately to fall back upon the laws of nature and of nature's God alone. In their name they declared their independence, and rejected the authority of Parliament as that of a body foreign to their constitution and unacknowledged by their laws.

For totally different reasons men of widely divergent views had combined to secure an immediate common end. Independence was achieved through a temporary alliance of mutually conflicting principles. In part it represented an attempt to transfer the sovereign attributes of Parliament to the legislatures of the several colonies; in part it was an effort to replace unpopular by popular sovereignty; in part it was a denial of any theory of absolute sovereignty in the name of an overruling law. Independence achieved, the work of reconstruction, of replacing one form of government by another, made clear this hostility of principles. United in resistance men became aware that they were yet divided in opinion. "An *elective despotism*," wrote Jefferson in his Notes on Virginia, "was not the government we fought for, but one which should not only be founded on free principles, but in which the powers of government should be so divided and balanced among several bodies of magis-

tracy, as that no one could transcend their legal limits, without being effectually checked and restrained by the others." But it was precisely such a despotism that many now feared; and the struggle over the new state governments, and the experience of their working under the weak union of the Confederation, confirmed or inspired in many an American mind an invincible distrust of democracy. In part, no doubt, this was a distrust born of turbulence, and the fear of the subversion of all government. Gerry, in the Federal Convention, confessed that "he had been too republican heretofore; he was still, however, republican, but had been taught by experience the danger of the levelling spirit." The bright democratic faith of some was dimmed. The Federal Constitution was in part a remarkably successful effort on the part of the propertied classes to stop revolution at a point at which it became dangerous for themselves.

That there is much truth in this judgment cannot be denied. But it is not the whole truth. If, as Acton said, "the authors of the most celebrated Democracy in history esteemed that the most formidable dangers which menaced the stability of their work were the very principles of Democracy itself," they cannot therefore be dismissed simply as reactionaries. For the very *fons et origo* of the revolution had been the belief in a controlling rule of law, a mistrust of absolutism as such. That the people were the source of political authority, that they had rights anterior to all government, these were doctrines on which few would dare to take issue. "British liberties," said John Adams, were "not the grants of princes or parliaments, but original rights, conditions of original contracts, coequal with prerogative, and coeval with government." In founding a new government, he declared, it was necessary to "realize the theories of the wisest writers, and invite the people to erect the whole building with their own hands, upon the broadest foundation." If these, as he avers, were "new, strange and terrible doctrines to the greatest part" of those who heard him, "not a very small number heard them with apparent pleasure." On these principles at least John Adams and his great rival, Thomas Jefferson, were agreed; never throughout their lives did Adams or Jefferson deny them. But not therefore were democratic governments omnipotent and absolute.

Jefferson, indeed, had leanings towards absolutism. The faith in the "steady and rational character of the American people" burned clearly within him. The dead, he felt, had no right to control the living. Every constitution and every law ought naturally to expire at the end of nineteen years. "After all," he declared, "it is my principle that the will of the majority should always prevail." But yet, he was to say in his Inaugural, that will, to be rightful, must be reasonable. And perhaps Jefferson would not have endorsed all majority wills. Natural rights and bills of rights were close to his heart. After all, it was not an elective despotism he had fought for, "but one which should not only be founded on free principles, but in which the powers of government should be . . . divided and balanced."

Jefferson's strength did not lie in his logic and political philosophy. Adams, on the other hand, was the ablest political philosopher of his day; and the study of the development of his mind repays attention. It has been alleged that Adams changed his principles. "The bold champion of the Revolution" became "equally fearless in his advocacy of strong government and of aristocratic principles." But there was no inconsistency in John Adams's thought; there was merely logical development. "The fundamental article of

my political creed," he wrote in 1815, "is, that despotism, or unlimited sovereignty, or absolute power, is the same in a majority of a popular assembly, an aristocratical council, an oligarchical junto, and a single emperor." And what was fundamental to Adams in 1815 was also fundamental in 1775.

Always a constitutional lawyer, Adams had come to perceive the necessity of independence reluctantly enough. In his opposition to the sovereign authority of Parliament, he would have been "very happy," as he remarked in his Autobiography, "if the constitution could carry us safely through all our difficulties without having recourse to higher powers, not written." He appealed exhaustively to precedent. But he was quite prepared to resort to higher powers, not written, should the necessity arise. He was clear that the authority which Parliament claimed was contrary both to constitutional and natural law, and that the law of nature was the foundation of rights in general, of the British constitution in particular, and indeed of all just government. Government, he declared was a "plain, simple, intelligible thing, founded in nature and reason, and quite comprehensible by common sense." But the common sense view of the matter did not lead Adams to the conclusion that because by natural law men had equal rights, because government rested on the consent of the governed, that therefore a majority should have the power to trample on a minority. On the contrary, as he remarked to Jefferson in 1798, "as to trusting to a popular assembly for the preservation of our liberties it was the merest chimera imaginable, they never had any rule of decision but their own will."

There was the crux of the matter. How was it possible to maintain a controlling rule of law? That was the question which Adams had in mind in 1815, in 1798, and in 1775. The basis of government must admittedly be broad; but its powers must be confined. A good government said Adams, in the words of Harrington, must be an empire of laws. Ecclesiastical controversies, he alleges in his Autobiography, had quite early helped to show him "in all their dismal colours, the deceptions to which the people in their passions are liable." He had, he affirms, small respect for that "popular talk" and "those democratical principles which have done so much mischief in this country." And a circumstantial and amusing story relates his alarm at the "spirit" and "principles" which the revolution had engendered. Adams's faith in the steady and rational character of the American people grew weaker rather than stronger; and these observations may not reflect contemporary states of mind at all. But his reflections on government in 1775 and 1776 reveal a mind already made up on the fundamental principles of liberty and constitutional organization. "A legislative, an executive, and a judicial power," he wrote, "comprehend the whole of what is meant and understood by government. It is by balancing each of these powers against the other two, that the efforts in human nature towards tyranny can alone be checked and restrained, and any degree of freedom preserved in the constitution." Adams had been attacking absolutism, but to no purpose if that absolutism was to be replaced by another nearer home. "A people," he wrote, "cannot be long free, nor ever happy whose government is in one assembly."

These principles Adams ever retained and developed. "It is a fixed principle with me," he wrote in 1790, "that all good government is and must be republican." The people must have "collectively, or by representation, an essential share in the sovereignty." But the "multitude" must also "have a check." "Power," he declared, "is always abused when unlimited and unbalanced." For "since all men are so inclined to act according to their own wills and interests in making, expounding, and executing laws, to the prejudice of the people's liberty and security, the sovereign authority, the legislative, executive, and judicial power, can never be safely lodged in one assembly, though chosen annually by the people; because the majority and their leaders, the *principes populi,* will as certainly oppress the minority . . . as hereditary kings or standing senates."

To Adams, then, sovereignty must be limited and divided, checked and balanced. The only true sovereign was the law and the constitution. Adams, in short, attacked not the absolutism of a given body at a given time, but of any body at any time. The experience of the revolution and its aftermath confirmed his belief in the principles with which he set out. The law of nature, the rule of right and reason, whose ultimate authority he continued to exalt, meant for him that in human institutions and constitutions must be enshrined a rule of law to preserve the natural rights of men against the tyranny either of majorities or minorities. A republic must be an empire of laws, not of men.

In 1957 CAROLINE ROBBINS (b. 1903), professor of English history at Bryn Mawr College, published *The Eighteenth-Century Commonwealthman*. In it she described a body of English dissenting political thought which she suggested, and subsequent scholarship has demonstrated, was central to the American revolutionary experience. Is it possible that the revolutionary generation could have found as much inspiration in the spirit as in the content of these political writings?*

Caroline Robbins

The English Libertarian Heritage

"A True Whig is not afraid of the name of a Commonwealthsman, because so many foolish People who know not what it means, run it down." This often-quoted definition proudly claimed for the Real Whigs—as they liked to call themselves—kinship with luminaries of republican thought like Milton, Harrington, Sidney, and others. In the eighteenth century the majority of the ruling oligarchy and the greater part of their fellow countrymen emphatically denied any continuity or connection between the innovators and Levellers of the Puritan Revolution (1641–1660), and the philosophers and Whiggish statesmen of the struggle (1679–1710) to exclude James Stuart and

secure the Glorious Revolution.[1] An eccentric antiquarian might hang a copy of Charles the First's execution writ in his closet and speak slightingly of kings and superstitions, but in general all talk of '41

---

[1] Historical note: In July 1642 the armies of Parliament and King Charles I, second in the line of Stuart kings, went to war. In January 1647 Charles was captured by Parliamentary forces and two years later beheaded. For the next eleven years England lived under the Commonwealth, experimenting with varying republican forms of government. In 1660, however, the Stuarts regained the throne, first in the person of Charles II (1660–1685) and then James II (1685–1688). Finally, in the Glorious Revolution of 1688–1689 James II was ousted, William and Mary (the first of the Hanoverian monarchs) were installed, and the constitutional reforms of the Revolutionary Settlement were enacted.—Ed.

---

*Reprinted by permission of the publishers from Caroline Robbins, *The Eighteenth-Century Commonwealthman*. Cambridge, Mass.: Harvard University Press. Copyright, 1959, by the President and Fellows of Harvard College. Passages selected by the editor from pp. 3–21. Footnotes omitted.

alarmed Englishmen as much or more than the sight of Jacobite toasts "over the water." Any proposed tampering with the fabric of the church and state produced dismal recollections and dire predictions.

The Commonwealthmen were only a fraction of politically conscious Britons in the Augustan Age, and formed a small minority among the many Whigs. No achievements in England of any consequence can be credited to them. English development shows scarcely a trace of efforts to restore or amend the mixed or Gothic government they esteemed. Their continued existence and activity, albeit of a limited kind, served to maintain a revolutionary tradition and to link the histories of English struggles against tyranny in one century with those of American efforts for independence in another. The American constitution employs many of the devices which the Real Whigs vainly besought Englishmen to adopt and in it must be found their abiding memorial. . . .

The natural rights doctrines of the Real Whigs formed an amalgam of theories drawn from several periods. Experience and history revealed the possibilities and the dangers of violent upheavals. The Commonwealthmen shared some of the conservatism of their contemporaries and much of the general misunderstanding of the nature and development of the ancient constitution. They had no difficulty in reconciling the rule of the Hanoverians with the precepts of classical republicans. They hoped to preserve and enlarge the merits of the "Gothic" system under which they thought they were living. They saw in the "rota" and separation of powers advocated by men like Harrington and Moyle useful and possible reforms which would secure liberty. Between them and other Englishmen differences were always more violently articulated than their extent would

seem to demand. The Commonwealthmen could be regarded as the conservators of the older order; they must also be seen as the spiritual heirs and ancestors of revolutionaries everywhere.

Three generations of Commonwealthmen will be described. . . . The first appeared not long after the Revolution of 1689 and most of its members were dead by 1727; the second grew to manhood during the mid-eighteenth century and brought up the third generation of the age of the American Revolution. . . .

The association of the eighteenth-century Commonwealthmen with the Levellers and republicans embittered controversy by suggesting that such Whigs could not be good subjects. We may admit the ancestry of their ideas without endorsing the accusations recalled in sermons commemorating the execution of Charles I on every thirtieth of January. The Whigs cherished ideas about checks on government from within and without, about individual freedoms and about the ranks of society, as we must later discuss, but their inheritance of the revolutionary tradition was tempered by the admiration for the English Constitution which they shared with nearly all their contemporaries. All Whigs until the French Revolution maintained that in theory at least tyrants could be resisted, and by so doing, justified the events of 1689. This was their chief advantage over Tories like Bolingbroke and Hume who accepted the Revolution without a logical defense for it. But even amongst the greatest admirers of Sidney and Milton, few promoted reform through violent means. Resistance rights, in fact, were only exercised by the Jacobites or by an occasional rioter. . . .

The Commonwealthmen saw in the development of Cabinet government a threat to the balance of the constitution. They believed in a separation of powers and hoped that each of the three parts of the government [King, Lords, and Commons] would balance or check the others. They fully recognized that ministerial predominance could be as dangerous as monarchical. They, therefore, wished to separate legislative and executive branches more completely, and roundly condemned placemen and party cliques and cabals. . . .

Reform of parliament by a wider franchise and some redistribution of seats removing anomalies like Old Sarum[2] was urged throughout the century by Real Whigs. Molesworth suggested enfranchisement of leaseholders. Hutcheson and Campbell would have allowed all men of property to vote. By 1780 Brand Hollis and his associates were advocating manhood suffrage. Members would be brought in closer touch with public opinion. Commonwealthmen, however, favoured the selection as members of parliament of those rich enough to be independent of bribes. They were vociferous advocates of annual parliaments, this expedient securing one kind of rotation. Management of the Commons, always resented by all factions out of office, was particularly offensive to the Real Whigs who heaped abuse on Walpole and ignored the possibility that he understood the public temper at least as well as they.

The Real Whigs greatly extended the application of general statements of right so frequent in English constitutional pronouncements. Two such principles were vigorously expressed in the works of Molyneux, Molesworth, Fletcher, and Trenchard, which were entirely denied by most contemporary politicians. One of these insisted that an Englishman was entitled to

be ruled by laws to which he had himself consented, wherever he was, at home or abroad, and the other extended this right to all mankind. The first claim would have meant considerable modification of mercantilist theory, an absolute denial of the rights of the English, or British, House of Lords to determine cases arising in Ireland, and, in general, extension of the powers of bodies like the Irish parliament, or, as time went on, colonial legislatures. . . .

The second principle extended the rights of Englishmen to all mankind. The right of conquest was no longer recognized. Conquest did not, according to these men, confer rights of long duration, nor did it deprive the conquered of their privileges as human beings. . . . In many ways the most enduring influence of the Commonwealthmen may be found in their emphasis, for many different reasons, upon the rights of the less privileged sections of society and of the British dominions. These "Whigs" did not forget Milton's admonition to remind Englishmen of their precedence of teaching nations how to live.

Another topic constantly discussed amongst the Real Whigs was freedom of thought. This was by no means confined to the agitation of the dissenters—still an oppressed, though prosperous and diminishing, minority—for fuller religious liberty and equal political status. The question of the Jews was raised. Discussion can be found amongst members of the Established Church who hoped for such changes in its discipline and dogma as would allow of greater freedom amongst its members and might induce a wider degree of conformity to it by those then outside it. . . .

Constant discussions of religious liberty were significant for at least two reasons: reiteration of a need for greater toleration and the development among Christians of a less ferocious dogmatism. The idea of a state in which no one was more privileged

---

[2]A once thriving borough near present-day Salisbury which, by the eighteenth century, contained virtually no population but continued to return several members to Parliament.—Ed.

than another because of his religion nor in any way penalized for his lack of orthodoxy was kept before the people in tracts, sermons, treatises. The Real Whigs had very early advocated a tolerance which went far beyond the theories of Locke or Milton. Molesworth and Toland included in its scope Jews, Atheists, Unitarians, Mohammedans, and even well-behaved Catholics, though it was not until Priestley's time that many were convinced that papists were also to benefit in the right of freedom of religion. The Commonwealthman kept before the public the Whig tradition of toleration in spite of the fact that the ruling oligarchy—under Walpole in a position of greater power than any party had ever enjoyed—never conceded anything but a meagre financial dole to the demands of dissent. . . .

Lively controversy in the realm of theology as well as reiterated demands for an untrammeled freedom of enquiry may well be admitted to have been an important contribution of this section of the Whigs. This admission does not, however, answer the question whether these Commonwealthmen were egalitarian or levelling in any real sense of the term. The answer must be sought in several directions. A great deal about attitudes toward social classes and inequality of privilege may be discovered in contemporary examination of the function of the charity schools. Closely connected with this, and very often to be found in the same sermons or tracts, were investigations into the ranks of society and their different duties in the state. With this last question was associated some consideration of wealth and its possible redistribution which, in turn, was closely linked with the fear of undue luxury. A shift in the balance of property and an excessive indulgence in the pleasures it could bring were matters of the deepest interest to many.

A great many people who were in no sense of the word egalitarian accepted ideas about human nature derived from Locke and Shaftesbury. Man's virtue or character was the product of education and environment. The third earl of Shaftesbury modified this theory by the belief that a moral sense within man would enable him—if not prevented by adverse circumstance or environment—to discover the laws of nature and to attain virtue. In the long run the influence of such theories was to lead Frenchmen to an emphasis on equality, but in England the chief influence of the philosophers was outside practical politics. Discussion about charity schools is illustrative of this.

The controversy is familiar. It is no less important than the questions raised by thoughtful men in Ireland over mercantilist restrictions. Would not, in the long run, the general welfare of the British Isles be raised by increasing the possibility of the acquisition of wealth in all the parts? Would allowing Irish manufacture of wool ruin England's economy? Was it to the advantage of the whole community to have all ranks of society educated? If all classes were educated would there not be none to perform the laborious tasks by which the wealth of society was produced, and would not all, therefore, become poorer? Such questions were endlessly debated. I will illustrate only from the work of two men whose ideas are those of the Commonwealthmen: Isaac Watts, the hymn writer who died in 1748, and Robert Wallace, an acquaintance of Hume, who died in 1771.

Both men believed the charity schools performed a useful function in training good Protestant citizens. In arguing for more than the minimum of education against those who distrusted the experiment, Watts put forward the notion that the poor but clever boy should not be denied the use of his talents even if by so doing he advanced his social position. Wallace was led further to a discussion as to whether it was necessary at all to condemn the majority of mankind to drudgery and whether some division of such labours could not be discovered. As the century went on there were not wanting radicals who suggested that education should be provided for all. Though agreeing with this, Priestley was to betray nervousness over possible government interference with individual freedom should the schools be state-endowed.

The manner of education raised questions about the inequalities of society which were solved more dogmatically in France by her revolutionary philosophers than in England. Equality was never a battle cry during the Civil War and Interregnum, although egalitarian speculations occasionally found written or spoken expression. That men might ideally share all in common as the apostles were once supposed to have done was the wish of small groups of men. These men on the whole, like Lilbourne and Winstanley, belong in that Christian tradition of which More's *Utopia* was still the most important English document. A very small section only believed such a community of property practicable. The eighteenth-century Levellers, as their critics called our Whigs, read tracts propounding these ideas. . . . Property, its definition and the position its owners enjoyed in the state were constantly examined. A few of the Commonwealthmen—Francis Hutcheson and Mrs. Macaulay for example—supported so-called "agrarian laws" for a moderate limitation of wealth.

The suggestion of an agrarian law in the eighteenth century did not spring from any drastic desire to distribute wealth more evenly in an endeavour to make the real condition of man more consonant with the ideal equality he enjoyed at birth. Support of the Agrarian stemmed from a belief that too great an accumulation of wealth in a few hands might disturb the balance of the state. Men like Edward Wortley Montagu (or the writer who used his name) in his *Rise and Fall of Antient Republicks,* and John Brown in his *Estimate,* as well as some Irish observers, found in the existence of luxury a danger to society, to morale, and to the survival of the nation. A few men at the end of the eighteenth century put forward ideas which appear socialist in character, but these seem to have had little connection either with the Commonwealthmen of their own day or with the literature of the Interregnum.

On the whole, the Real Whig was not egalitarian although he might emphasize to an embarrassing degree the equality of man before God, or in a state of nature. A ruling class and an uneducated and unrepresented majority were for a long time taken for granted. Most of these Whigs wanted to provide education, to increase religious liberty, and were willing to recognize the political rights of all those who, through the acquisition of property, should be qualified as citizens. By "people" most seventeenth-century Republicans had meant people of some state and consequence in the community. Cobblers, tinkers, or fishermen were not people but *scum* to Whigs like James Tyrrell—who used the term—to Locke, Withers, and Trenchard. Constant discussion of the greatest good of the greatest number, and an optimistic interpretation of the workings of an untrammeled moral sense eventually brought about an attitude of mind which made it impossible to justify deprivation of the means of exercising and developing human potentialities. I doubt whether many of the later Whigs of any kind in the eighteenth century expressed, much less endorsed, what might appear to be modern democratic ideas brought forward from time to time in the parliaments of a century before. . . .

Until the great parliamentary researches now proceeding are complete, it will be difficult to say how many of the self-styled Real Whigs found their way into parliament. There were probably very few, though their ideas may have found expression during election contests. Candidates may have made speeches full of anti-monarchical and revolutionary sentiments—for the benefit not only of voters but of the crowds at large—which failed to influence their actions once they were elected to the House. Many contests passed with little local excitement, but even septennial parliamentary changes served to stir up political debates. A certain disgust with the revered institution of the House of Commons is noticeable. Men like Thomas Hollis refused even to vote. Christopher Wyvill worked for reform through extra-parliamentary association. Parliament afforded very little opportunity for the discussion of their ideas. Even if these ideas gained some public support, this by no means insured effective action in the divisions. Commonwealthmen relied therefore on other means of disseminating the principles they held—teachers and textbooks, clubs and coteries, correspondence, domestic and foreign, preachers and publications, both of the classical Republicans and of periodical and polemical treatises. . . .

A gifted and active minority of the population of the British Isles continued to study government in the spirit of their seventeenth-century ancestors. They kept alive, during an age of extraordinary complacency and legislative inactivity, a demand for increased liberty of conscience, for an extension of the franchise and for a re-examination of the distribution of parliamentary seats. They discussed rotation in office, the separation of powers, and such expedients as the Ephors or Conservators recommended by Ludlow and Moyle, which would guard the balance of the different parts of the constitution and preserve it from corruption. They considered the relations of different parts of the old empire to each other. Men like Molesworth, Fletcher, Trenchard and Pownall made suggestions which included equal or federal union between the different parts of the British Isles and a partnership or family compact between Britain and her distant colonies. They achieved no major success in the period. The radicals and liberals of the nineteenth century paid some lip service to their reputation and their efforts, but in fact their utilitarian assumptions did not emphasize the old natural rights doctrines and their political conceptions ignored the forms and theories of the mixed government earlier generations had esteemed. Where both Commonwealthman and liberal shared a distrust of too powerful a government the one relied upon a due balance between its different component parts, the other sought a release of individuals from statutory restrictions and controls as preservatives against the Leviathan state.

In the constitutions of the several United States many of the ideas of the Real Whigs found practical expression. A supreme court, rotation in office, a separation of powers, and a complete independence from each other of church and state fulfilled many a so-called utopian dream. The endless opportunities of the New World brought about a considerable degree of social equality, if not an equality stabilized by an agrarian law. The democratical element in the state was much extended. Neither in the New nor the Old World was the widely held ideal of a partyless government achieved. In the new republic of the West nearly all the other aspirations of the classical republicans or Real Whigs found a measure of fulfillment which would have astounded and delighted them could they have lived to see this.

Morgan argued that the Revolution brought to completion a profound shift in the categories of American thought—from religious to predominantly political modes of self-definition. PERRY MILLER (1905–1963), at his death Powell M. Cabot Professor of American Literature at Harvard, takes direct issue with Morgan's assertion. In his most famous work, *The New England Mind,* Miller traces out the elaboration of Puritan thought during the first century of New England's existence. In an article from which the following selection is taken, he extends his analysis into the revolutionary period. Throughout history, virtually every society has claimed divine mandate for its actions. Is the historian, given his peculiar tasks and kinds of evidence, in a position to say anything about the validity of such claims? In trying to determine the importance of religious belief for an understanding of revolutionary thought, one must be careful not to impose one's own values and preconceptions upon the people whose thought is under study.*

Perry Miller

Religion as Revolutionary Ideology

On June 12, 1775, the Continental Congress dispatched from Philadelphia to the thirteen colonies (and to insure a hearing, ordered the document to be published in newspapers and in handbills) a "recommendation" that July 20 be universally observed as "a day of publick humiliation, fasting, and prayer." The Congress prefaced the request with a statement of reasons. Because the great "Governor" not only conducts by His Providence the course of nations "but frequently influences the minds of men to serve the wise and gracious purposes of his providential government," and also it being our duty to acknowledge his superintendency, "especially in times of impending danger and publick calamity"—therefore the Congress acts.

What may elude the secular historian—what in fact has eluded him—is the mechanism by which the Congress proposed that the operation be conducted:

... that we may with united hearts and voices unfeignedly confess and deplore our many sins, and offer up our joint supplications to the all-wise, omnipotent, and merciful Disposer of all events; humbly beseeching him to for-

*"From the Covenant to the Revival," by Perry Miller, pp. 322–343, without footnotes in *The Shaping of American Religion,* Vol. I of *Religion in American Life,* eds. James Ward Smith and A. Leland Jamison (Princeton University Press, 1961). Reprinted by permission of Princeton University Press.

give our iniquities, to remove our present calamities, to avert those desolating judgments with which we are threatened. . . .

The essential point is that the Congress asks for, first, a national confession of sin and iniquity, then a promise of repentance, that only *thereafter* may God be moved so to influence Britain as to allow America to behold "a gracious interposition of Heaven for the redress of her many grievances." The subtle emphasis can be detected once it is compared with the formula used by the Virginia House of Burgesses in the previous month, on May 14:

> . . . devoutly to implore the Divine interposition for averting the heavy calamity which threatens destruction to our civil rights, and the evils of civil war, to give us one heart and one mind firmly to oppose, by all just and proper means, every injury to *American* rights. . . .

Jefferson testifies that in Virginia this measure was efficacious. The people met with alarm in their countenances, "and the effect of the day through the whole colony was like a shock of electricity, arousing every man and placing him erect and solidly on his centre." However gratifying the local results might be, it should be noted that this predominantly Anglican House of Burgesses, confronted with calamity, made no preliminary detour through any confession of their iniquities, but went directly to the throne of God, urging that He enlist on their side. The Virginia delegation in Philadelphia (which, let us remember, included Patrick Henry but *not* Jefferson) concurred in the unanimous adoption of the Congress's much more complicated—some were to say more devious—ritualistic project. Was this merely a diplomatic concession? Or could it be that, once the threatened calamity was confronted on a national scale, the assembled representatives of all the peoples instinctively realized that some

deeper, some more atavistic, search of their own souls was indeed the indispensable prologue to exertion?

The question is eminently worth asking, if only because conscientious historians have seen no difference between the two patterns, and have assumed that the Congressional followed the Virginian. And there are other historians, who may or may not be cynical, but who have in either case been corrupted by the twentieth century, who perceive in this and subsequent summonses to national repentance only a clever device in "propaganda." It was bound, they point out, to cut across class and regional lines, to unite a predominantly Protestant people; wherefore the rationalist or deistical leaders could hold their tongues and silently acquiesce in the stratagem, calculating its pragmatic worth. In this view, the fact that virtually all the "dissenting" clergy, and a fair number of Anglicans, mounted their pulpits on July 20 and preached patriotic self-abnegation, is offered as a proof that they had joined with the upper middle-class in a scheme to bamboozle the lower orders and simpleminded rustics.

This interpretation attributes, in short, a diabolical cunning to the more sophisticated leaders of the Revolution, who, being themselves no believers in divine providence, fastened onto the form of invocation which would most work upon a majority who did believe passionately in it. This reading may, I suggest, be as much a commentary on the mentality of modern sociology as upon the Continental Congress, but there is a further observation that has been more cogently made by a few who have noted the striking differences in phraseology: the Congressional version is substantially the form that for a century and a half had been employed in New England. There, since the first years of

Plymouth and the first decade of Massachusetts Bay and Connecticut, the official response in the face of affliction had been to set aside a day for public confession of transgression and a promise of communal repentance as the only method for beseeching the favor of Jehovah. Hence some analysts surmise that the action of the Congress, if it was not quite a Machiavellian ruse for hoodwinking the pious, was at best a Yankee trick foisted on Virginia and New York. Leaving aside the question of whether, should this explanation be true, it might just as well have been a Virginian fraud, one which cost Patrick Henry and Peyton Randolph nothing, perpetrated to keep the New Englanders active, the simple fact is that unprejudiced examination of the records of 1775 and 1776 shows that New England enjoyed no monopoly on the procedure. The House of Burgesses might suppose it enough to petition Almighty God to redress their wrongs; the churches of the dissenters, and indeed most Anglican communities already knew, whether in Georgia, Pennsylvania, or Connecticut, that this was not the proper way to go about obtaining heavenly assistance. The Biblical conception of a people standing in direct daily relation to God, upon covenanted terms and therefore responsible for their moral conduct, was a common possession of the Protestant peoples.

However, there can be no doubt that New England had done much more than the other regions toward articulating colonial experience within the providential dialectic. Because, also, presses were more efficient there than elsewhere, and Boston imprints circulated down the coast, it is probable that the classic utterances of Massachusetts served as models for Presbyterians and Baptists as well as for "low-church" Anglicans. For many decades the Puritan colonies had been geographically set apart; the people had been thoroughly accustomed to conceiving of themselves as a chosen race, entered into specific covenant with God, by the terms of which they would be proportionately punished for their sins. Their afflictions were divine appointments, not the hazards of natural and impersonal forces. Furthermore, the homogeneity of the Puritan communities enabled their parsons to speak in the name of the whole body—even when these were internally riven by strife over land banks, the Great Awakening, or baptism. Finally, this same isolation of the New England colonies encouraged a proliferation of the "federal theology" to a point where the individual's relation with God, his hope of salvation through a personal covenant, could be explicitly merged with the society's covenant. Hence in New England was most highly elaborated the theorem that the sins of individuals brought calamity upon the commonwealth.

In that sense, then, we may say that the Congressional recommendation of June 12, 1775, virtually took over the New England thesis that these colonial peoples stood in a contractual relation to the "great Governor" over and above that enjoyed by other groups; in effect, Congress added the other nine colonies (about whose status New Englanders had hitherto been dubious) to New England's covenant. Still, for most of the population in these nine, no novelty was being imposed. The federal theology, in general terms, was an integral part of the Westminster Confession[1] and so had long figured in the rhetoric of Presbyterians of New Jersey and Pennsylvania. The covenant doctrine, including that of the society as well as of the individual, had been preached in the founding of Virginia,

[1] Passed by Parliament in 1660 during the English Civil War, giving a Presbyterian constitution to the Church of England and introducing uniformity of doctrine, worship, and order.—Ed.

and still informed the phraseology of ordinary Anglican sermonizing. The Baptists, even into Georgia, were aware of the concept of church covenant, for theirs were essentially "congregational" polities; they could easily rise from that philosophy to the analogous one of the state. Therefore the people had little difficulty reacting to the Congressional appeal. They knew precisely what to do: they were to gather in their assemblies on July 20, inform themselves that the afflictions brought upon them in the dispute with Great Britain were not hardships suffered in some irrational political strife but intelligible ordeals divinely brought about because of their own abominations. This being the situation, they were to resolve, not only separately but in unison, to mend their ways, restore primitive piety, suppress vice, curtail luxury. Then, and only thereafter, if they were sincere, if they proved that they meant their vow, God would reward them by raising up instruments for the deflection of, or if necessary, destruction of, Lord North.

Since the New Englanders were such old hands at this business—by exactly this method they had been overcoming, from the days of the Pequot War through King Philip's War, such difficulties as the tyranny of Andros, smallpox epidemics, and parching droughts—they went to work at once. For the clergy the task was already clear: beginning with the Stamp Act of 1765, the clerical orator who spoke at every election day, in May, surveyed the respects in which relations with England should be subsumed under the overall covenant of the people with God. Charles Chauncy's *A Discourse on the good News from a far Country,* delivered upon a day of "thanksgiving" (the logical sequel to several previous days of humiliation) to the General Court in 1766, explained that repeal of the odious Stamp Act was a consequence not of any mercantile resistance but of New England's special position within the Covenant of Grace. As the crisis in Boston grew more and more acute, successive election orators had an annual opportunity to develop in greater detail proof that any vindication of provincial privileges was inextricably dependent upon a moral renovation. Following the "Boston Massacre" of 1773, anniversaries of this atrocity furnished every preacher an occasion for spreading the idea among the people. The form of these discourses was still that of the traditional "jeremiad"—a threatening of further visitation upon the covenanted people until they returned to their bond by confession and reformation—but by the time the Congress issued its wholesale invitation, the New England clergy had so merged the call to repentance with a stiffening of the patriotic spine that no power on earth, least of all the government of George III, could separate the acknowledgment of depravity from the resolution to fight.

Everything the Congress hoped would be said in 1775 had already been declared by the Reverend Samuel Cooke of the Second Church in Boston at the election of 1770. If that were not precedent enough, the General Court on October 22, 1774, confronting General Gage and the Boston Port Bill, showed how double-edged was the sword by proclaiming not a fast day but one of thanksgiving; it was illuminated by the sermon of William Gordon, from the Third Church in Roxbury, which was all the more memorable because Gordon had been English-born. On May 31, 1775, six weeks after Lexington and Concord, Samuel Langdon, President of Harvard, put the theory of religious revolution so completely before the Court (then obliged to meet in Watertown) that the doctrine of political resistance yet to be formulated in the Declaration seems but an afterthought.

A few weeks before that assertion, on May 29, 1776, Samuel West of Dartmouth made clear to the General Court that what was included within the divine covenant as a subsidiary but essential portion had been not simply "British liberties" but the whole social teaching of John Locke. After the evacuation of Boston, both Massachusetts and Connecticut were able to assemble as of old, and comfortably listen to a recital of their shortcomings, secure in the knowledge that as long as jeremiads denounced them, their courage could not fail. The fluctuations of the conflict called for many days of humiliation and a few for thanksgiving; in Massachusetts, the framing of the state constitution in 1780 evoked another spate of clerical lectures on the direct connection between piety and politics. Out of the years between the Stamp Act and the Treaty of Paris[2] emerged a formidable, exhaustive (in general, a repetitious) enunciation of the unique necessity for America to win her way by reiterated acts of repentance. The jeremiad, which in origin had been an engine of Jehovah, thus became temporarily a service department of the Continental army.

The student of New England's literature is not astonished to find this venerable machine there put to patriotic use; what has not been appreciated is how readily it could be set to work in other sections. On this day of humiliation, July 20, 1775, Thomas Coombe, an Anglican minister at Christ's Church and St. Peter's in Philadelphia, who once had been chaplain to the Marquis of Rockingham, explained, in language which would at once have been recognized in Connecticut, that our fast will prove ineffectual unless we execute a genuine reformation of manners (interestingly enough, the printed text is dedicated to Franklin):

------

[2] 1763, ending The Seven Years' War.—Ed.

We must return to that decent simplicity of manners, that sober regard to ordinances, that strict morality of demeanor, which characterized our plain forefathers; and for the decay of which, their sons are but poorly compensated by all the superfluities of commerce. We must *associate* to give a new tone and vigor to the drooping state of religion among ourselves. We must support justice, both public and private, give an open and severe check to vices of every sort, and by our example discourage those luxurious customs and fashions, which serve but to enervate the minds and bodies of our children; drawing them off from such manly studies and attainments, as alone can render them amiable in youth or respectable in age.

This Philadelphia Anglican combined as neatly as any Yankee the call for patriotic resistance and the old cry of Cotton Mather that the people respond to a jeremiad by implementing *Essays To Do Good.* By Coombe's standard, Quaker Philadelphia would appear to be a Babylon, but the opportunity for salvation was at last providentially offered: "Let such persons, however, now be told, that patriotism without piety is mere grimace."

Thus we should not be surprised that Jacob Duché, preaching on this same July 20 before not only his Anglican parish but the assembled Congress, portrayed the whole trouble as "a national punishment" inflicted on "national guilt." He surveyed, as did all "Puritan" speakers, the manifest favors God had shown the colonies, and then diagnosed their present affliction as centering not on the iniquity of the British Cabinet (iniquitous as it undoubtedly was) but rather on the infidelity of Americans:

... have we not rather been so far carried away by the stream of prosperity, as to be forgetful of the source from whence it was derived? So elevated by the prospect, which peace and a successful commerce have opened to us, as to neglect those impressions of goodness, which former affections had left upon our hearts.

Was it not palpably for this reason, and this alone, "that the Almighty hath bared his arm against us?" If so, the answer for Duché, as for President Langdon, was clear: by reformation of manners, by a return to primitive piety, we would, as a united people, win the cause of American liberty. "Go on, ye chosen band of Christians," he cried to the Congress. The fact that after the Declaration Duché lost heart and turned Loyalist does not make his *The American Vine* any less a spiritual jeremiad of the sort that most invigorated Patriot courage. . . .

If anywhere among the states the lineaments of Puritan federal theology would be dim, one might suppose that place to be Charleston, South Carolina. Legend continually obscures for us, however, how profoundly Protestant the culture of that region was at this time and for several decades afterwards. In 1774 William Tennent, son of the great William of Log College, expounded to planters and merchants that they were threatened with slavery because of their transgressions. The first dictate of natural passion is to imprecate vengeance upon the instruments of our torment, to resolve to endure hardships rather than surrender the privileges of our ancestors. But this, Tennent explained, is the wrong procedure. The first duty of good men is to find out and bewail "the Iniquities of our Nation and country," which are the true causes of the dismal catastrophe about to befall us.

Though by now the Revolution has been voluminously, and one might suppose exhaustively, studied, we still do not realize how effective were generations of Protestant preaching in evoking patriotic enthusiasm. No interpretation of the religious utterances as being merely sanctimonious windowdressing will do justice to the facts or to the character of the populace. Circumstances and the nature of the dominant opinion in Europe made it necessary for the official statement to be released in primarily "political" terms—the social compact, inalienable rights, the right of revolution. But those terms, in and by themselves, would never have supplied the drive to victory, however mightily they weighed with the literate minority. What carried the ranks of militia and citizens was the universal persuasion that they, by administering to themselves a spiritual purge, acquired the energies God had always, in the manner of the Old Testament, been ready to impart to His repentant children. Their first responsibility was not to shoot redcoats but to cleanse themselves; only thereafter to take aim. Notwithstanding the chastisements we have already received, proclaimed the Congress on March 20, 1779—they no longer limited themselves to mere recommending—"too few have been sufficiently awakened to a sense of their guilt, or warmed with gratitude, or taught to amend their lives and turn from their sins, so He might turn from His wrath." They call for still another fast in April, 1780: "To make us sincerely penitent for our transgressions; to prepare us for deliverance, and to remove the evil with which he hath been pleased to visit us; to banish vice and irreligion from among us, and establish virtue and piety by his Divine grace." And when there did come a cause for rejoicing (almost the only one in four or five years that might justify their using other vestibule, the surrender of Burgoyne), patriots gave little thought to lengthening lines of supply or the physical obstacles of logistics; instead they beheld Providence at work again, welcomed Louis XVI[3] as their "Christian ally," and congratulated themselves upon that which had really produced victory—their success in remodeling themselves. Now more than

---

[3] King of France, 1774–1792.—Ed.

ever, asserted the Congress on October 31, 1777, we should "implore the mercy and forgiveness of God, and beseech him that vice, profaneness, extortion and every evil may be done away, and that we may be a reformed and a happy people."

Historians of English political thought have reduced to a commonplace of inevitable progression the shift of Puritan political philosophy from the radical extreme of 1649 to the genial universals of 1689. John Locke so codified the later versions as to make the "Glorious Revolution" seem a conservative reaction. As we know, Locke was studied with avidity in the colonies; hence the Congress used consummate strategy in presenting their case to a candid world through the language of Locke.

Nevertheless, we do know that well before the Civil War began in England, Parliamentarians—and these include virtually all Puritans—had asserted that societies are founded upon covenant; that the forms of a particular society, even though dictated by utilitarian factors, are of divine ordination; that rulers who violate the agreed-upon forms are usurpers and so to be legitimately resisted. This complex of doctrine was transported bodily to early Virginia and most explicitly to Puritan New England.... Governor Winthrop[4] was not much troubled, though possibly a bit, when he told the men of Hingham that in signing the covenant they had agreed to submit to rulers set over them for their own good—unless they could positively prove that their rulers were the violators!

The development of New England, however, steadily encouraged the citizens to deduce that they themselves, in framing the compact, had enumerated the items which made up their good. John Cotton and John Winthrop, having entirely ac-

cepted the contractual idea, were still making within it a last-ditch stand for medieval scholasticism by contending that the positive content of the magisterial function had been prescribed by God long before any specific covenant, whether of Israel or of Massachusetts, was drawn up. By the mid-eighteenth century, even in "semi-Presbyterial" Connecticut, good Christians were certain they could designate both the duties and the limitations of magistrates. In basically similar fashion, though not so easily traceable, the same transformation was wrought among the Protestant, or at least among the "Calvinistic," elements of all the communities. To put the matter bluntly, the agitation which resulted in the War for American Independence commenced after an immense change had imperceptibly been wrought in the minds of the people. That they needed from 1765 to 1776 to realize this was not because they had, under stress, to acquire the doctrine from abroad, but because they did have to search their souls in order to discover what actually had happened within themselves.

Consequently, every preacher of patriotism was obliged to complicate his revolutionary jeremiad by careful demonstrations of exactly how the will of almighty God had itself always operated through the voluntary self-imposition of a compact, how it had provided for legitimate, conservative resistance to tyrants. Early in the eighteenth century, John Wise prophesied how this union of concepts would be achieved, but he seems to have had no direct effect on the patriot argument. Jonathan Mayhew was far ahead of his fellows; after his death in 1766 the others required hard work to catch up. In general it may be said that they started off serenely confident that of course the philosophy of the jeremiad, which required abject confession of unworthiness from an afflicted people, and that of the social compact, which called for immediate and vigor-

---

[4] First governor of the Massachusetts Bay colony.—Ed.

ous action against an intruding magistrate, were one and the same. Then, discovering that the joining required more carpentry than they had anticipated, they labored for all they were worth at the task. Finally, by 1776, they triumphantly asserted that they had indeed succeeded, that the day of humiliation was demonstrably one with the summons to battle.

Political historians and secular students of theory are apt to extract from the context those paragraphs devoted solely to the social position, to discuss these as comprising the only contribution of the "black regiment" to Revolutionary argument. To read these passages in isolation is to miss the point. They were effective with the masses not as sociological lectures but because, being embedded in the jeremiads, they made comprehensible the otherwise troubling double injunction of humiliation and exertion. In this complicated pattern (which could be offered as the ultimate both in right reason and in true piety), the mentality of American Protestantism became so reconciled to itself, so joyfully convinced that it had at last found its long-sought identity, that for the time being it forgot that it had ever had any other reason for existing.

A few examples out of thousands will suffice. Gordon's *Discourse* of December 15, 1774, runs for page after page in the standardized jeremiad vein: "Is not this people strangely degenerated, so as to possess but a faint resemblance of that godliness for which their forefathers were eminent?" Is it not horrible beyond all imagination that *this* people should degenerate, seeing how scrupulously God has befriended them according to the stipulations of their covenant with Him? Yet the ghastly fact is "that while there is much outward show of respect to the Deity, there is but little inward heart conformity to him." And so on and on, until abruptly, with hardly a perceptible shift, we are hearing a recital of the

many palpable evidences that Divine Providence is already actively engaged in the work. Only by the direct "inspiration of the Most High" could the unanimity of the colonies have been brought about. From this point Gordon's cheerful jeremiad comes down to the utilitarian calculation that Americans are expert riflemen, wherefore "the waste of amunition will be greatly prevented"; after which he concludes by urging the people to "accept our punishment at his hands without murmuring or complaining"!

The elements woven together in this and other speeches can, of course, be separated one from another in the antiseptic calm of the historian's study, and the whole proved to be an unstable compound of incompatible propositions. What may be left out of account is the impact of the entire argument, the wonderful fusion of political doctrine with the traditional rite of self-abasement which, out of colonial experience, had become not what it might seem on the surface, a failure of will, but a dynamo for generating action.

President Langdon's sermon of May, 1775 played a slight variation on the theme by suggesting that the notorious crimes of England had brought these troubles as a divine visitation on *her!* Other preachers occasionally toyed with this device, but obviously it was not the full-throated note the populace expected and wanted. Langdon returned to the really effective music when he justified the afflictions of America:

But alas! have not the sins of America, and of New England in particular, had a hand in bringing down upon us the righteous judgments of Heaven? Wherefore is all this evil come upon us? Is it not because we have foresaken the Lord? Can we say we are innocent of crimes against God? No surely.

After several pages of such conventional self-accusation, the moral emerges as easily in 1775 as it used to flow from the mouth of Cotton Mather: "However unjustly and cruelly we have been treated by man, we certainly deserve, at the hand of God, all the calamities in which we are now involved."

Then follows a turn which is indeed novel, which reveals the subtle yet largely unconscious transformation that the Revolution was actually working in the hearts of the people. Langdon concludes his jeremiad by calling upon Americans to repent and reform, because *if* true religion can be revived, "we may hope for the direction and blessing of the most High, while we are using our best endeavors to preserve and restore the civil government of this colony, and defend America from slavery."

Here, in exquisite precision, is the logic of the clerical exhortation which, though it may seem to defy logic, gives a vivid insight into what had happened to the pious mentality of the communities. For, Langdon's argument runs, once we have purged ourselves and recovered our energies in the act of contrition, how then do we go about proving the sincerity of our repentance (and insuring that Divine Providence will assist us)? We hereupon act upon the principles of John Locke! At this point, and not until after these essential preliminaries, Langdon turns to his exposition of Whig doctrine:

Thanks be to God that he has given us, as men, natural rights, independent of all human laws whatever, and that these rights are recognized by the grand charter of British liberties. By the law of nature, any body of people, destitute of order and government, may form themselves into a civil society according to their best prudence, and so provide for their common safety and advantage. When one form is found by the majority not to answer the grand purpose in any tolerable degree, they may, by common consent, put an end to it and set up another.

The next year, Samuel West of Dartmouth persuaded the General Court of Massachusetts, not to mention readers elsewhere in the colonies, that the inner coherence of the thesis was maintained by these two combined doctrines: while, because of our abysmally sinful condition, we must obey magistrates for conscience' sake, we also find "that when rulers become oppressive to the subject and injurious to the state, their authority, their respect, their maintenance, and the duty of submitting to them, must immediately cease; they are then to be considered as the ministers of Satan, and as such, it becomes our indispensable duty to resist and oppose them." What we today have to grasp is that for the masses this coalescence of abnegation and assertion, this identification of Protestant self-distrust with confidence in divine aid, erected a frame for the natural-rights philosophy wherein it could work with infinitely more power than if it had been propounded exclusively in the language of political rationalism.

There were, it should be pointed out, a few clerics who could become patriots without having to go through this labyrinth of national humiliation. But in the colonies they were a minority, and they came from a Protestantism which had never been permeated by the federal theology—which is to say, they were generally Anglicans. . . .

The really effective work of the "black regiment" was not an optimistic appeal to the rising glory of America, but their imparting a sense of crisis by revivifying Old Testament condemnations of a degenerate people. . . .

What aroused a Christian patriotism that needed staying power was a realization of the vengeance God denounced against the wicked; what fed their hopes was not what God promised as a recompense to virtue, but what dreary fortunes would overwhelm those who persisted in sloth; what kept them going was an assurance that by exerting themselves they were fighting for a victory thus providentially predestined.

To examine the Revolutionary mind from the side of its religious emotion is to gain a perspective that cannot be acquired from the ordinary study of the papers of the Congresses, the letters of Washington, the writings of Dickinson, Paine, Freneau, or John Adams. The "decent respect" that these Founders entertained for the opinion of mankind caused them to put their case before the civilized world in the restricted language of the rational century. A successful revolution, however, requires not only leadership but receptivity. Ideas in the minds of the foremost gentlemen may not be fully shared by their followers, but these followers will accept the ideas, even adopt them, if such abstractions can be presented in an acceptable context. To accommodate the principles of a purely secular social compact and a right to resist taxation—even to the point of declaring political independence to a provincial community where the reigning beliefs were still original sin and the need of grace—this was the immense task performed by the patriotic clergy.

Our mental image of the religious patriot is distorted because modern accounts do treat the political paragraphs as a series of theoretical expositions of Locke, separated from what precedes and follows. When these orations are read as wholes, they immediately reveal that the sociological sections are structural parts of a rhetorical pattern. Embedded in their contexts, these are not abstractions but inherent parts of a theology. It was for this reason that they had so energizing an effect upon their religious auditors. The American situation, as the preachers saw it, was not what Paine presented in *Common Sense*—a community of hard-working, rational creatures being put upon by an irrational tyrant—but was more like the recurrent predicament of the chosen people in the Bible. As Samuel Cooper declared on October 25, 1780, upon the inauguration of the Constitution of Massachusetts, America was a new Israel, selected to be "a theatre for the display of some of the most astonishing dispensations of his Providence." The Jews originally were a free republic founded on a covenant over which God "in peculiar favor to that people, was pleased to preside." When they offended Him, He punished them by destroying their republic, subjecting them to a king. Thus while we today need no revelation to inform us that we are all born free and equal and that sovereignty resides in the people— "these are the plain dictates of that reason and common sense with which the common parent has informed the human bosom"—still Scripture also makes these truths explicit. Hence when we angered our God, a king was also inflicted upon us; happily, Americans have succeeded, where the Jews did not, in recovering something of pristine virtue, whereupon Heaven redressed America's earthly grievances. Only as we today appreciate the formal unity of the two cosmologies, the rational and the Biblical, do we take in the full import of Cooper's closing salute to the new Constitution: "How nicely it poises the powers of government, in order to render them as far as human foresight can, what God ever designed they should be, power only to do good."

PETER GAY (b. 1923), professor of modern European history at Yale University, has written extensively on European intellectual history, particularly of the seventeenth and eighteenth centuries. In this essay he explores some of the relationships between Enlightenment thought in America and in Europe. Note that he finds more of interest in the revolutionary generation's approach to political problem-solving (he labels it "pragmatic rationalism") than in the content of their ideas.*

Peter Gay

Enlightenment Thought and the American Revolution

To compare the American with the European Enlightenment is a risky business, not because they have nothing in common—they have in fact a great deal in common—but because they are not of the same logical order. The Enlightenment was a great revolution in man's style of thinking that came to dominate the Western world in the eighteenth century. It was composed of the interplay among ideas and events, inventions and expectations; its raw materials were the triumph of Newtonian science, striking improvements in industrial and agricultural techniques, a widespread loss of religious fervor and a corresponding rise of "reasonable" religion, an ever bolder play of the critical spirit among the old mysteries of church and state which had for centuries escaped criticism, a new sense of confidence in man's power over his wordly destiny. The *philosophes* in many areas, including the British colonies in America, articulated and organized these developments into a coherent philosophy and made it into a set of demands, a full-fledged political program. In this enterprise, each area had its part to play; each was at once unique and tied to the others as a member of a family. The American Enlightenment was one such member, prominent though not of the first rank, in the family of the Western Enlightenment; it can be properly compared only with other individuals in that family—the Scottish, say, or the Genevan Enlightenment.

*From Chapter 3, "The Enlightenment" by Peter Gay, in *The Comparative Approach to American History* edited by C. Vann Woodward, © 1968 by C. Vann Woodward, Basic Books, Inc., Publishers, New York.

Yet the traditional procedure of comparing the American with the whole European Enlightenment has persisted in both major schools of thought among American historians, both among those who regard the American Enlightenment as a pernicious myth and those who regard it as a glorious reality. It has persisted because these two schools of historians, for all their differences, share an almost unqualified admiration for what, in short, I want to call the American *philosophes*—the politician-intellectuals who led the revolution and rationalized it, drafted the Constitution and governed the young country. The first school sees Franklin, Jefferson, and their fellows as statesmen so practical that they did not need theories, or even ideas, and steered clear, with unspoiled instinct, of the treacherous rocks of European ideologies. The second school sees Franklin, Jefferson, and their fellows as thinkers indeed, but as tough-minded realistic thinkers who managed to discard the fantasies of European theoreticians.

Both these interpretations misstate the relation of theory to practice, ideas to experience, and, worse, the relation of America to Europe; both are a direct consequence of compressing the variety of the European experience into a specious unity. Each local enlightenment, whether American or French or Lombard, generated, transformed, and echoed certain ideas, and each modified its ideas through its particular experience. The commitment to practicality, on which Americans have often thought they hold a monopoly, is after all itself an idea, an idea in fact with a long and honored history. Precisely like the *philosophes* in France or England and following their lead, the American *philosophes* acquired their respect for practicality from a close reading of the Roman classics. Cicero especially was for all *philosophes* everywhere a model of the thoughtful statesman; he

was the philosopher in politics. In addition, the Americans learned to value practicality by studying the attacks on metaphysics and what was derisively called "system-making" launched by Locke and Newton, justified by Hume and Condillac, and popularized by Voltaire and d'Alembert. Like the other *philosophes*, the Americans got some of their respect for practicality from being practical men, much of it from being readers. What made the American *philosophes* distinctive was not that they were realists while their English and French brethren were dreamers, but rather that their particular experience taught them lessons different from the lessons that experience taught the *philosophes* in Scotland or France or Milan. Fortunately for the Americans, the American experience included the winning of a revolution which gave them a captive audience for their ideas. . . . The relations of *philosophes* to their state and their society differed in country after country; but the difference was not one of varying degrees of practicality, it was one of power. Whereas in the European countries vested interests managed to defeat, absorb, or partially to honor the demands of the *philosophes*, in America the *philosophes* became the vested interest; they were compelled to be practical: their good fortune forced them to test their ideas in sober reality.

It should therefore surprise no one that the American *philosophes* sounded in most respects precisely like their European brethren. If anyone has had the reputation of a Utopian in Europe, it was Condorcet. In his *Essay on the Progress of the Human Mind*, written in hiding from the Jacobins in 1793–1794, Condorcet forecast a future in which the further improvement of the natural sciences and the establishment of the social sciences would bring to all men an enviable existence, with substantial equality, high standards of living, and a life indefinitely prolonged and freed from anxiety and disease. Among the Americans, it became fashionable to ridicule Condorcet's naïve hopes, though Jefferson for one professed to agree with Condorcet's trust in human perfectibility. But Benjamin Franklin, who has become a byword for realism, accepted and in fact anticipated Condorcet's brilliant picture of the future. "The rapid Progress *true* Science now makes," he wrote to Priestley in 1780, "occasions my regretting sometimes that I was born so soon. It is impossible to imagine the Height to which may be carried, in a thousand years, the Power of Man over Matter. We may perhaps learn to deprive large Masses of their Gravity, and give them absolute Levity, for the sake of easy Transport. Agriculture may diminish its Labour and double its Produce; all Diseases may by sure means be prevented or cured, not excepted even that of Old Age, and our Lives lengthened at pleasure even beyond the antediluvian Standards." To be sure, there was one area in which man showed as yet little progress: "O that moral Science were in as fair a way of Improvement, that Men would cease to be Wolves to one another, and the human Beings would at length learn what they now improperly call Humanity!" But this wistful qualification, this distinction between material and moral progress, was a commonplace among the Scottish, French, and German *philosophes,* and in fact deeply troubled Condorcet himself: the French Utopian was not so naïve, the American Realist not so skeptical, it seems, as has often been supposed. To say, as Adrienne Koch has said, that "the French Enlightenment, in all its brilliant achievements and rich profusion of doctrines and dogmas, did not cast up the kind of sagacious and flexible leadership that came to the highest places of power in the American Revolution and in the ensuing years of

Confederation and Constitutional Republic" is to underestimate both what *philosophes* all over the Western world had in common and the opportunities which the American *philosophes* had for displaying their sagacity.

Since the unique dimension of the American Enlightenment was its preparation for revolution, the Revolution, and what it did with the Revolution, the special claim of the American Enlightenment to historical distinction must lie in the decades of the 1760s, 1770s and 1780s. Properly enough, Koch dates the American Enlightenment from 1765 to 1815. But by 1765, *philosophes* from Edinburgh to Milan, London to Berlin, had completed the structure of scientific, aesthetic, social, religious, and political ideas that constitute the Enlightenment. In the making of these ideas, for all of Franklin's reputation as a scientist, the American colonists had no part. The period before 1765 was the prehistory of the American Enlightenment; in this period the Americans were consumers, depending heavily, almost exclusively, on borrowings from overseas. To be sure, not all was dependence; like the others, the American *philosophes* developed their particular intellectual style by listening to domestic developments in Boston or Philadelphia or Richmond or the frontier that lay just beyond. But just as the American Puritans had shaped their ideas by following the course of events and the evolution of thinking among English Dissenters, so the American *philosophes,* most of them still young men before 1765, went to school to a handful of European thinkers.

This dependence of America on Europe is easy to document in detail, for the Americans never thought of concealing it. Benjamin Franklin formed his style on Addison's *Spectator,* found his way into deism by reading English religious controversy, perfected his scientific knowledge by studying English Newtonians. He attributed his turn toward humanitarianism to a reading of Cotton Mather's *Essays to Do Good,* but he minimizes this single concession to local pride almost as soon as he has made it by mentioning, in the same breath, Defoe's *Essay on Projects.* John Adams, though contemptuous of the "naïve optimism" of Helvétius and Rousseau, developed his theory of lawful revolution by close study of the legal writings of Grotius, Pufendorf, Barbeyrac, and other European lawyers, shaped his political outlook by close study of Harrington, Locke, Montesquieu, and other European political theorists, and sought for an adequate theory of human nature by close study of Hutcheson, Ferguson, Bolingbroke, and other European philosophers. Adams made much—and much has been made since—of his disagreements with European "dreamers," but then Adams liked developing his own thought in opposition; and besides, even if he rejected some European *philosophes,* he rejected them in the name, and with the aid, of other European *philosophes.* Jefferson was notoriously dependent on Europe. Adams' comment, malicious in intent, that Jefferson "drank freely of the French philosophy, in religion, in science, in politics," is not so much inaccurate as it is incomplete; Jefferson was open to his Virginian experience and drank as freely from English as he did from French thought, and more freely from English than from French literary models. It is well known that he called Bacon, Newton, and Locke his "trinity of the three greatest men the world had ever seen"—a trinity, we should note, not merely *of* Europeans, but worshiped by Europeans; it was precisely the trinity adored by Voltaire, d'Alembert, Hume, Lichtenberg, and Kant. Jefferson was, like the British *philosophes,* a Francophile; and he was, like the French and

German *philosophes,* an Anglomaniac. Madison's political thought, in turn, is inexplicable without reference to the Scottish Enlightenment and Montesquieu's political ideas. Madison was, much like Franklin, a disciple of Addison, and echoed Voltaire's Anglomania in Voltaire's very words. Alexander Hamilton stands a little isolated from this group, with his admiration of monarchy and—if we may believe Jefferson—for Julius Caesar; but he made it perfectly plain that he had drawn his political principles from such unimpeachable European sources as Grotius, Pufendorf, Locke, and Montesquieu, and that he claimed to abhor—in good European fashion—that most impeachable of European theorists, Hobbes. Hamilton's rhetoric, and I think his political program, was that of the European Enlightenment; tender words like "reason" and "humanity" punctuate his most tough-minded pronouncements, and not as flourishes alone.

What holds true of these giants holds true of the less celebrated figures. As Bernard Bailyn has shown, the American radicals who from the early 1760s on began to wonder out loud whether the colonies could continue to live under the tyranny of a corrupt British homeland drew their arguments almost exclusively from Europe. Jonathan Mayhew, James Otis, John Dickinson, and the others larded their pamphlets with ideas—and sometimes plagiarized long passages—from Scottish and English, French and Milanese *philosophes,* from English common lawyers, and above all from English republicans of the seventeenth and eighteenth centuries: Milton, Harrington, Sidney, Trenchard, Gordon, and that much maligned, much underestimated Latitudinarian prelate, Bishop Hoadly. Indeed, it was this last group, with their cohorts, who represented to the American rebels the sum of modern political wisdom. England, it was clear, had the

best constitution man had ever devised—
the mixed constitution—and if it became
necessary to rebel it was only because England was now departing from this glorious
invention; England, it seemed, must be
rescued from herself. In sum, there can be
no doubt: in the formation of the American Enlightenment European thinkers
played a decisive part, and American *philosophes* were apt and candid disciples.

Disciples often apply their lessons a generation late, and their finest productions
may bear the character of an anachronism.
So it was in the American Enlightenment:
the Declaration of Independence, which
must always remain the most celebrated
production of the American Enlightenment, is, from the philosophical point of
view, a reminder of arguments that were
losing their respectable status. At a time
when European thinkers were turning to
Utilitarianism, the declaration persisted in
employing the logic of natural law: as
everyone knows, it justified separation by
appealing to "the laws of nature," and to
"nature's God," and to "self-evident"
truths. But by 1776, Hume, Helvétius,
Beccaria, and Bentham had thrown serious doubts on the possibility of discovering
moral laws of nature; had discarded God,
even nature's God; and had denied self-
evident truths outside of mathematics.
Natural law and natural rights remained
good battle cries: Tom Paine and Condorcet used them to the end, and so did the
authors of the French Declaration of the
Rights of Man. Locke's political ideas—at
least as simplified by his hasty readers—retained their usefulness long after they had
been riddled by criticism. The Declaration
of Independence, a disciple's production,
exhibits that usefulness by disregarding
these criticisms.

I insist on this point here not to pa-
tronize the Declaration of Independence,
but to characterize the relation of American to English, Scottish, and French
thought. After all, the declaration was a
political rather than a philosophical document, and it was, on its own terms supreme-
ly successful. It was clear, circumstantial,
dignified, and persuasive. And it was more
than that; the Declaration of Independence is a symbol of the shift of the American Enlightenment from consumer to pro-
ducer, from importer to exporter, a shift
that became manifest in the 1770s. Now
what the American Enlightenment exported was, of course, first of all itself. America became the model for Europeans of
good hope—living, heartening proof that
men had a capacity for growth, that reason
and humanity could become governing
rather than merely critical principles. America was, to be sure, a model that pointed
in two opposite directions at once; admirers of primitive simplicity could call on it
just as much as could admirers of refined
civilization. And this duality was the secret
of Benjamin Franklin's enormous success
as a missionary of the American cause: he
seemed to embody both the virtues of nature and the triumphs of civility; he was—
or rather, in his shrewdness, enormously
enjoyed playing—the savage as philosopher. David Hume, no primitivist and
not given to excesses of flattery, was en-
chanted with this commodity exported by
the American Enlightenment. "America
has sent us many good things," he wrote to
Franklin, "gold, silver, sugar, tobacco, in-
digo, etc., but you are the first philosopher,
and indeed the first great man of letters,
for whom we are beholden to her." John
Adams, who did not much like Franklin,
was half amused, half irritated, to discover
in Paris in 1779 that Franklin was widely
considered a universal genius, "another
Voltaire and Hume," and the "great Philosopher and the great Legislator of America," as well as a great wit. These were

claims that Adams felt constrained to dispute, but the tribute paid to Franklin by Europe was more than a personal tribute: it was expression of the great hope that the ideas of the Enlightenment might become reality. And later, as the American colonies gained their independence, survived the tests of the first years, and succeeded in transcending parochialism in that magnificent compromise, the Constitution of the United States, the myth that Franklin represented appeared to have, after all, a good deal of substance.

The American *philosophes* were not slow to celebrate their political sagacity. Madison especially, looking back, was fond of describing the American "experiment" as an "example of a free system," and he was confident that that system would be "more of a Pilot to a good Port, than a Beacon warning from a bad one." America had constructed a "great Political Machine," and as a result, the whole "Civilized World" had discovered the blessings of "Representative Government." Unquestionably, he insisted, the United States was the "workshop of liberty," and the people of the United States "enjoy the great merit of having established a system of Government on the basis of human rights, and of giving to it a form without example"— America was new, it had no model but was a model to others. And even John Adams, who had little trust in human nature and whose political thought increasingly turned away from equality and freedom to devices for social control, felt constrained to admit that America had been splendid: "The last twenty-five years of the last century," he wrote in 1815, "and the first fifteen years of this, may be called the age of revolutions and constitutions. We began the dance . . ."

We can understand the reasons for this self-congratulation without wholly sharing it; if America began the dance, it was Scots and Englishmen and Frenchmen who had designed the figures for it. Yet there is some reality in these claims; the historical role of the young United States seemed to be to act as a laboratory for Enlightenment ideas. Now it is precisely at this point that the task of comparative history becomes exceedingly complicated; we need much further work to understand just how much the political ideals of the young republic owed to the ideas of the Enlightenment, how much to the improvisation of the moment, how much to ideas of sound administration that any sensible man in the eighteenth century would have applied, Enlightenment or no Enlightenment. It is certain that the colonies were good soil for the ideas of the European Enlightenment; a relatively long period of peace, and new conditions for work, had brought the colonists experiences in self-government, peaceful cooperation, and class mobility that were unavailable back in Europe. "Most of the legislation," Felix Gilbert has said, "which the *philosophes* in Europe advocated, had become a reality in America," and so there were some fights the American *philosophes* did not need to fight, or could fight with good prospects of success. This holds true even if we are constrained to admit, with skeptics like Leonard Levy, that under the pressure of events, from sheer intellectual confusion and the kind of helplessness that believing in one's own cant always produces, the Americans often behaved less creditably as statesmen than they had sounded as *philosophes*.

But in what, precisely, does the Enlightened quality of the American experiment consist? It lies, I think, in what I should like to call its "pragmatic rationalism." This quality has been, paradoxically enough, obscured by the ranting of articulate Americans against the French Revolution, and, later, by historians wrongly associating Americans with Burke. The leading American *philosophes* in fact rejected the cardinal principle of Burke's conservatism: that a constitution cannot be made, but must grow. John Adams, early and late, thought politics a "divine science," and was confident that men could discover "principles of political architecture." He cautioned, to be sure, that this architecture was "an art or mystery very difficult to learn, and still harder to practice," but after all, the Americans had learned and practiced it, so it was not on principle impossible. The authors of the *Federalist Papers*—and it is this document rather than the Declaration of Independence that strikes me as the most characteristic product of the American Enlightenment—distinguished between Utopian political blueprints and sensible political machines, but they never doubted that the state could be made into a successful mechanism promoting freedom while repressing the anarchy of passion. Madison's favorite phrase, "political experiment," deserves to be given its full weight: just as men learned from history—which was, as it were, a record book of both unsuccessful and successful experiments—so men could learn from present experience, as a physicist learns in the laboratory. The prevalence of bad machines, and the difficulty of devising good machines, did not deter the American *philosophes* from striving to become Newtonians of statesmanship—precisely the thing that Burke denounced as supreme, impious folly. It was this hardheaded confidence in the cooperation of reason with experience—a confidence which Madison and Adams shared with Voltaire and Kant—that produced the hardheaded optimism of the American *philosophes* which, once again, they shared with their brethren in Europe. It was an optimism that survives, indeed incorporates, a relatively low estimate of human nature. Much—too much, I think—has been made of the Calvinist, or Hobbesian, pessimism of the founding fathers. Like most of the *philosophes* in Europe, the founding fathers believed that passion is ruthless and undirected, and that the lower orders, guided by passion, lack the political wisdom to make the political machine work. Institutions, therefore, are the public superego, designed to restrain the passionate will and guide it into productive paths. The science of freedom required repression—for the sake of freedom. The mixing of constitutional elements, the balancing of political forces—ideas taken from classical political theory, modern political sociology, and Newtonian imagery—was, the founding fathers expected, the method that would provide the salutary mixture of freedom and control. If there was optimism, then, it rested on the conviction that America was essentially an experiment—pragmatic rationalism and ultimate optimism are two sides of the same principle. Writing to Count Sarsfield in 1786, John Adams expressed this conjunction with particular felicity: "It has ever been my hobby horse," he wrote, "to see rising in America an empire of liberty, and a prospect of two or three hundred millions of freemen, without one noble or one king among them. You say it is impossible. If I should agree with you in this"—and it is obvious that he does not—"I would still say, let us try the experiment." This temper—realistic yet hopeful, scientific but humanist, respectful but secular, trusting in institutions yet treating them as provisional, and looking to the day when all men are autonomous—it the link that ties the American Enlightenment to its colleagues in Scotland and England and France and Prussia; for it is the authentic, the characteristic temper of the Western Enlightenment as a whole.

Has the main theme of American history been class and group conflict or general agreement on matters of social and political philosophy? American historians have debated the question endlessly, and no one has contributed more importantly to the argument than LOUIS HARTZ, professor of political science at Harvard. In *The Liberal Tradition in America,* he stresses the basic Lockean premises underlying the main structure of American political thought. His ideas have obvious implications for any study of the American Revolution, for the reader must decide whether the revolutionary generation was in agreement or was sharply divided over matters of political ideology. Is it possible for men to argue heatedly, even violently, while sharing many of the same philosophical premises?*

Louis Hartz

John Locke and the Liberal Consensus

"The great advantage of the American," Tocqueville once wrote, "is that he has arrived at a state of democracy without having to endure a democratic revolution. . . ." Fundamental as this insight is, we have not remembered Tocqueville for it, and the reason is rather difficult to explain. Perhaps it is because, fearing revolution in the present, we like to think of it in the past, and we are reluctant to concede that its romance has been missing from our lives. Perhaps it is because the plain evidence of the American revolution of 1776, especially the evidence of its social impact that our newer historians have collected, has made the comment of Tocqueville seem thoroughly enigmatic. But in the last analysis, of course, the question of its validity is a question of perspective. Tocque-

ville was writing with the great revolutions of Europe in mind, and from that point of view the outstanding thing about the American effort of 1776 was bound to be, not the freedom to which it led, but the established feudal structure it did not have to destroy. He was writing too, as no French liberal of the nineteenth century could fail to write, with the shattered hopes of the Enlightenment in mind. The American revolution had been one of the greatest of them all, a precedent constantly appealed to in 1793. In the age of Tocqueville there was ground enough for reconsidering the American image that the Jacobins had cherished.

Even in the glorious days of the eighteenth century, when America suddenly became the revolutionary symbol of

---

*Louis Hartz, "American Political Thought and the Revolution," *American Political Science Review,* XLVI (1952), 321–342. All footnotes except two omitted.

Western liberalism, it had not been easy to hide the free society with which it started. As a matter of fact, the liberals of Europe had themselves romanticized its social freedom, which put them in a rather odd position. . . . If America was from the beginning a kind of idyllic state of nature, how could it suddenly become a brilliant example of social emancipation? Two consolations were being extracted from a situation which could at best yield only one. But the mood of the Americans themselves, as they watched the excitement of Condorcet seize the Old World, is also very revealing. They did not respond in kind. They did not try to shatter the social structure of Europe in order to usher in a Tenth and Final Epoch in the history of man. Delighted as they were with the support that they received, they remained, with the exception of a few men like Paine and Barlow, curiously untouched by the crusading intensity we find in the French and the Russians at a later time. Warren G. Harding, arguing against the League of Nations, was able to point back at them and say, "Mark you, they were not reforming the world." And James Fenimore Cooper, a keener mind than Harding, generalized their behavior into a comment about America that America is only now beginning to understand: "We are not a nation much addicted to the desire of proselytizing."

There were, no doubt, several reasons for this. But clearly one of the most significant is the sense that the Americans had themselves of the liberal history out of which they came. In the midst of the Stamp Act struggle, young John Adams congratulated his colonial ancestors for turning their backs on Europe's class-ridden corporate society, for rejecting the "canon and feudal law." The pervasiveness of Adams' sentiment in American thought has often been discussed, but what is easily

overlooked is the subtle way in which it corroded the spirit of the world crusader. For this was a pride of inheritance, not a pride of achievement; and instead of being a message of hope for Europe, it came close to being a damning indictment of it. It saturated the American sense of mission, not with a Christian universalism, but with a curiously Hebraic kind of separatism. The two themes fought one another in the cosmopolitan mind of Jefferson, dividing him between a love of Europe and fear of its "contamination"; but in the case of men like Adams and Gouverneur Morris, the second theme easily triumphed over the first. By the time the crusty Adams had gotten through talking to politicians abroad, he had buried the Enlightenment concept of an oppressed humanity so completely beneath the national concept of a New World that he was ready to predict a great and ultimate struggle between America's youth and Europe's decadence. As for Morris, our official ambassador to France in 1789, he simply inverted the task of the Comintern agent. Instead of urging the French on to duplicate the American experience, he badgered them by pointing out that they could never succeed in doing so. "They want an American constitution," he wrote contemptuously, "without realizing they have no Americans to uphold it."

Thus the fact that the Americans did not have to endure a "democratic revolution" deeply conditioned their outlook on people elsewhere who did; and by helping to thwart the crusading spirit in them, it gave to the wild enthusiasms of Europe an appearance not only of analytic error but of unrequited love. Symbols of a world revolution, the Americans were not in truth world revolutionaries. . . .

When the Americans celebrated the uniqueness of their own society, they were on the track of a personal insight of the profoundest importance. For the nonfeudal world in which they lived shaped every aspect of their social thought: it gave them a frame of mind that cannot be found anywhere else in the eighteenth century, or in the wider history of modern revolutions.[1]

One of the first things it did was to breed a set of revolutionary thinkers in America who were human beings like Otis and Adams rather than secular prophets like Robespierre and Lenin. Despite the European flavor of a Jefferson or a Franklin, the Americans refused to join in the great Enlightenment enterprise of shattering the Christian concept of sin, replacing it with an unlimited humanism, and then emerging with an earthly paradise as glittering as the heavenly one that had been destroyed. The fact that the Americans did not share the crusading spirit of the French and the Russians, as we have seen, is already some sort of confirmation of this, for that spirit was directly related to the "civil religion" of Europe and is quite unthinkable without it. Nor is it hard to see why the liberal good fortune of the Americans should have been at work in the position they held. Europe's brilliant dream of an impending millennium, like the mirage of a thirst-ridden man, was inspired in large part by the agonies it experienced. When men have already inherited the freest society in the world, and

are grateful for it, their thinking is bound to be of a solider type. America has been a sober nation, but it has also been a comfortable one, and the two points are by no means unrelated. . . .

Behind the shining optimism of Europe, there are a set of anguished grievances; behind the sad resignation of America, a set of implicit satisfactions. One of these satisfactions, moreover, was crucially important in developing the sober temper of the American revolutionary outlook. It was the high degree of religious diversity that prevailed in colonial life. This meant that the revolution would be led in part by fierce Dissenting ministers, and their leadership destroyed the chance for a conflict to arise between the worldly pessimism of Christianity and the worldly ambitions of revolutionary thought. In Europe, especially on the Continent, where reactionary church establishments had made the Christian concept of sin and salvation into an explicit pillar of the *status quo,* liberals were forced to develop a political religion, as Rousseau saw, if only in answer to it. The Americans not only avoided this compulsion; they came close, indeed, to reversing it. Here, above all in New England, the clergy was so militant that it was Tories like Daniel Leonard who were reduced to blasting it as a dangerous "political engine," a situation whose irony John Adams caught when he reminded Leonard that "in all ages and countries" the church is "disposed enough" to be on the side of conservatism. Thus the American liberals, instead of being forced to pull the Christian heaven down to earth, were glad to let it remain where it was. They did not need to make a religion out of the revolution because religion was already revolutionary. . . .

Sir William Ashley, discussing the origins of the "American spirit," once remarked that "as feudalism was not trans-

---

[1] The term "feudal," of course, has a technical reference to the medieval period. What Tocqueville and Adams largely had in mind, and what I refer to here, is the decadent feudalism of the later period—the "corporate" society of Europe, as some historians of the eighteenth century have put it. It has often been noted that the nonexistence of a feudal tradition—save for scattered remnants of which most, to be sure, were abolished by the American revolution—has been the great distinguishing feature of American civilization. But no interpretation of American politics or American political thought has as yet been inspired by this observation.

planted to the New World, there was no need for the strong arm of a central power to destroy it." This is a simple statement, but, like many of Ashley's simple statements, it contains a neglected truth. For Americans usually assume that their attack on political power in 1776 was determined entirely by the issues of the revolution, when as a matter of fact it was precisely because of the things they were not revolting against that they were able to carry it through. The action of England inspired the American colonists with a hatred of centralized authority; but had that action been a transplanted American feudalism, rich in the chaos of ages, then they would surely have had to dream of centralizing authority themselves.

They would, in other words, have shared the familiar agony of European liberalism—hating power and loving it too. The liberals of Europe in the eighteenth century wanted, of course, to limit power; but confronted with the heritage of an ancient corporate society, they were forever devising sharp and sovereign instruments that might be used to put it down. Thus while the Americans were attacking Dr. Johnson's theory of sovereignty, one of the most popular liberal doctrines in Europe, cherished alike by Bentham and Voltaire, was the doctrine of the enlightened despot, a kind of political deism in which a single force would rationalize the social world. While the Americans were praising the "illustrious Montesquieu" for his idea of checks and balances, that worthy was under heavy attack in France itself because he compromised the unity of power on which so many liberals relied. Even the English Whigs, men who were by no means believers in monarchical absolutism, found it impossible to go along with their eager young friends across the Atlantic. When the Americans, closing their eyes to 1688, began to lay the axe to the concept

of parliamentary sovereignty, most of the Whigs fled their company at once.

A philosopher, it is true, might look askance at the theory of power the Americans developed. It was not a model of lucid exposition. The trouble lay with their treatment of sovereignty. Instead of boldly rejecting the concept, as Franklin was once on the verge of doing when he said that it made him "quite sick," they accepted the concept and tried to qualify it out of existence. The result was a chaotic series of forays and retreats in which a sovereign Parliament was limited, first by the distinction between external and internal taxation, then by the distinction between revenue and regulation, and finally by the remarkable contention that colonial legislatures were as sovereign as Parliament was. But there is a limit to how much we can criticize the Americans for shifting their ground. They were obviously feeling their way; and they could hardly be expected to know at the time of the Stamp Act what their position would be at the time of the first Continental Congress. Moreover, if they clung to the concept of sovereignty, they battered it beyond belief, and no one would confuse their version of it with the one advanced by Turgot or even by Blackstone in Europe. The meekness of the American sovereign testifies to the beating he had received. Instead of putting up a fierce and embarrassing battle against the limits of natural law and the separation of powers, as he usually did in the theories of Europe, he accepted those limits with a vast docility. . . .

The question, again, was largely a question of the free society in which the Americans lived. Nor ought we to assume that its impact on their view of political power disappeared when war and domestic upheaval finally came. Of course, there was scattered talk of the need for a "dictator," as Jefferson angrily reported in 1782; and until new assemblies appeared in most places, Committees of Public Safety had authoritarian power. But none of this went deep enough to shape the philosophic mood of the nation. A hero is missing from the revolutionary literature of America. He is the Legislator, the classical giant who almost invariably turns up at revolutionary moments to be given authority to lay the foundations of the free society. He is not missing because the Americans were unfamiliar with images of ancient history, or because they had not read the Harringtons or the Machiavellis and Rousseaus of the modern period. Harrington, as a matter of fact, was one of their favorite writers. The Legislator is missing because, in truth, the Americans had no need for his services. Much as they liked Harrington's republicanism, they did not require a Cromwell, as Harrington thought he did, to erect the foundations for it. Those foundations had already been laid by history.

The issue of history itself is deeply involved here. On this score, inevitably, the fact that the revolutionaries of 1776 had inherited the freest society in the world shaped their thinking in a most intricate way. It gave them, in the first place, an appearance of outright conservatism. We know, of course, that most liberals of the eighteenth century, from Bentham to Quesnay, were bitter opponents of history, posing a sharp antithesis between nature and tradition. And it is an equally familiar fact that their adversaries, including Burke and Blackstone, sought to break down this antithesis by identifying natural law with the slow evolution of the past. The militant Americans, confronted with these two positions, actually took the second. Until Jefferson raised the banner of independence, and even in many cases after that time, they based their claims on a philosophic synthesis of Anglo-American legal history and the reason of natural law. Blackstone,

the very Blackstone whom Bentham so bitterly attacked in the very year 1776, was a rock on which they relied.

The explanation is not hard to find. The past had been good to the Americans, and they knew it. Instead of inspiring them to the fury of Bentham and Voltaire, it often produced a mystical sense of Providential guidance akin to that of Maistre—as when Rev. Samuel West, surveying the growth of America's population, anticipated victory in the revolution because "we have been prospered in a most wonderful manner." The troubles they had with England did not alter this outlook. Even these, as they pointed out again and again, were of recent origin, coming after more than a century of that "salutary neglect" which Burke defended so vigorously. And in a specific sense, of course, the record of English history in the seventeenth century and the record of colonial charters from the time of the Virginia settlement provided excellent ammunition for the battle they were waging in defense of colonial rights. A series of circumstances had conspired to saturate even the revolutionary position of the Americans with the quality of traditionalism—to give them, indeed, the appearance of outraged reactionaries. "This I call an innovation," thundered John Dickinson, in his attack on the Stamp Act, "a most dangerous innovation."

Now here was a frame of mind that would surely have troubled many of the illuminated liberals in Europe, were it not for an ironic fact. America piled on top of this paradox another one of an opposite kind, and thus as it were, by misleading them twice, gave them a deceptive sense of understanding.

Actually, the form of America's traditionalism was one thing, its content quite another. Colonial history had not been the slow and glacial record of development that Bonald and Maistre loved to talk about. On the contrary, since the first sailing of the *Mayflower,* it had been a story of new beginnings, daring enterprises, and explicitly stated principles—it breathed, in other words, the spirit of Bentham himself. The result was that the traditionalism of the Americans, like a pure freak of logic, often bore amazing marks of anti-historical rationalism. The clearest case of this undoubtedly is to be found in the revolutionary constitutions of 1776, which evoked, as Franklin reported, the "rapture" of European liberals everywhere. In America, of course, the concept of a written constitution, including many of the mechanical devices it embodied, was the end-product of a chain of historical experience that went back to the Mayflower Compact and the Plantation Covenants of the New England towns: it was the essence of political traditionalism. But in Europe just the reverse was true. The concept was the darling of the rationalists—a symbol of the emancipated mind at work. . . .

But how then are we to describe these baffling Americans? Were they rationalists or were they traditionalists? The truth is, they were neither, which is perhaps another way of saying that they were both. For the war between Burke and Bentham on the score of tradition, which made a great deal of sense in a society where men had lived in the shadow of feudal institutions, made comparatively little sense in a society where for years they had been creating new states, planning new settlements, and, as Jefferson said, literally building new lives. In such a society a strange dialectic was fated to appear, which would somehow unite the antagonistic components of the European mind; the past became a continuous future, and the God of the traditionalists sanctioned the very arrogance of the men who defied Him.

This shattering of the time categories of Europe, this Hegelian-like revolution in

historic perspective, goes far to explain one of the enduring secrets of the American character: a capacity to combine rock-ribbed traditionalism with high inventiveness, ancestor worship with ardent optimism. Most critics have seized upon one or the other of these aspects of the American mind, finding it impossible to conceive how both can go together. That is why the insight of Gunnar Myrdal is a very distinguished one when he writes: "America is . . . conservative. . . . But the principles conserved are liberal and some, indeed, are radical." Radicalism and conservatism have been twisted entirely out of shape by the liberal flow of American history.

What I have been doing here is fairly evident: I have been interpreting the social thought of the American revolution in terms of the social goals *it did not need to achieve.* Given the usual approach, this may seem like a perverse inversion of the reasonable course of things; but in a world where the "canon and feudal law" are missing, how else are we to understand the philosophy of a liberal revolution? The remarkable thing about the "spirit of 1776," as we have seen, is not that it sought emancipation but that it sought it in a sober temper; not that it opposed power but that it opposed it ruthlessly and continuously; not that it looked forward to the future but that it worshipped the past as well. Even these perspectives, however, are only part of the story, misleading in themselves. The "free air" of American life, as John Jay once happily put it, penetrated to deeper levels of the American mind, twisting it in strange ways, producing a set of results fundamental to everything else in American thought. The clue to these results lies in the following fact: the Americans, though models to all the world of the middle class way of life, lacked the passionate middle class consciousness which saturated the liberal thought of Europe.

There was nothing mysterious about this lack. It takes the contemptuous challenge of an aristocratic feudalism to elicit such a consciousness; and when Richard Price glorified the Americans because they were men of the "middle state," men who managed to escape being "savage" without becoming "refined," he explained implicitly why they themselves would never have it. . . .

There can, it is true, be quite an argument over whether the challenge of an American aristocracy did not in fact exist in the eighteenth century. One can point to the great estates of New York where the Patroons lived in something resembling feudal splendor. One can point to the society of the South where life was extraordinarily stratified, with slaves at the bottom and a set of genteel planters at the top. One can even point to the glittering social groups that gathered about the royal governors in the North. But after all of this has been said, the American "aristocracy" could not, as Tocqueville pointed out, inspire either the "love" or the "hatred" that surrounded the ancient titled aristocracies of Europe. Indeed, in America it was actually the "aristocrats" who were frustrated, not the members of the middle class, for they were forced almost everywhere, even in George Washington's Virginia, to rely for survival upon shrewd activity in the capitalist race. This compulsion produced a psychic split that has always tormented the American "aristocracy"; and even when wealth was taken for granted, there was still, especially in the North, the withering impact of a colonial "character" that Sombart himself once described as classically bourgeois. In Massachusetts Governor Hutchinson used to lament that a "gentleman" did not meet even with "commom civility" from his inferiors. Of course, the radicals of America blasted their betters as "aristocrats," but that this was actually a subtle compliment is betrayed in the quality of the blast itself. . . .

Thus it happened that fundamental aspects of Europe's bourgeois code of political thought met an ironic fate in the most bourgeois country in the world. They were not so much rejected as they were ignored, treated indifferently, because the need for their passionate affirmation did not exist. . . .

But this is not all. If the position of the colonial Americans saved them from many of the class obsessions of Europe, it did something else as well: it inspired them with a peculiar sense of community that Europe had never known. For centuries Europe had lived by the spirit of solidarity that Aquinas, Bossuet, and Burke romanticized: an organic sense of structured differences, an essentially Platonic experience. Amid the "free air" of American life, something new appeared: men began to be held together, not by the knowledge that they were different parts of a corporate whole, but by the knowledge that they were similar participants in a uniform way of life—by that "pleasing uniformity of decent competence" which Crèvecoeur loved so much. The Americans themselves were not unaware of this. When Peter Thacher proudly announced that "simplicity of manners" was the mark of the revolutionary colonists, what was he saying if not that the norms of a single class in Europe were enough to sustain virtually a whole society in America? Richard Hildreth, writing after the levelling impact of the Jacksonian revolution had made this point far more obvious, put his finger directly on it. He denounced feudal Europe, where "half a dozen different codes of morals," often in flagrant contradiction with each other, flourished "in the same community," and celebrated the fact that America was producing "one code, one moral standard, by which the actions of all are to be judged. . . ." Hildreth knew that America was a marvellous mixture of many peoples and many regions, but he also knew that it was characterized by something more marvellous even than that: the power of the liberal norm to penetrate them all.

Now a sense of community based on a sense of uniformity is a deceptive thing. It looks individualistic, and in part it actually is. It cannot tolerate internal relationships of disparity, and hence can easily inspire the kind of advice that Professor Nettels once imagined a colonial farmer giving his son: "Remember that you are as good as any man—and also that you are no better." But in another sense it is profoundly anti-individualistic, because the common standard is its very essence, and deviations from that standard inspire it with an irrational fright. The man who is as good as his neighbors is in a tough spot when he confronts all of his neighbors combined. Thus William Graham Sumner looked at the other side of Professor Nettels's colonial coin and did not like what he saw: "public opinion" was an "impervious mistress. . . . Mrs. Grundy held powerful sway and Gossip was her prime minister."

Here we have the "tyranny of the majority" that Tocqueville later described in American life; here too we have the deeper paradox out of which it was destined to appear. Freedom in the fullest sense implies both variety and equality; but history, for reasons of its own, chose to separate these two principles, leaving the one with the old society of Burke and giving the other to the new society of Paine. America, as a kind of natural fulfillment of Paine, has been saddled throughout its history with the defect which this fulfillment involves, so that a country like England, in the very midst of its ramshackle class-ridden atmosphere, seems to contain an in-

definable germ of liberty, a respect for the privacies of life, that America cannot duplicate. At the bottom of the American experience of freedom, not in antagonism to it but as a constituent element of it, there has always lain the inarticulate premise of conformity, which critics from the time of Cooper to the time of Lewis have sensed and furiously attacked. . . .

One thing, we might suppose, would shatter the unprecedented sense of uniform values by which the colonial American was beginning to live: the revolution itself. But remarkably enough, even the revolution did not produce this result; John Adams did not confront Filmer, as Locke did, or Maistre, as the followers of Rousseau did. He confronted the Englishmen of the eighteenth century; and most of these men, insofar as the imperial struggle went, themselves accepted the Lockean assumptions that Adams advanced. Nor did the American Tories, with the fantastic exception of Boucher, who stuck to his thesis that Filmer was still "unrefuted," confront him with a vision of life completely different from his own. Samuel Seabury and Joseph Galloway accepted the Lockean principles, even sympathized with the American case, insisting only that peaceful means be used to advance it. Among their opponents, indeed, there were few who would fundamentally deny the "self-evident" truths the Americans advanced in 1776. The liberals of Europe always had a problem on their hands, which they usually neglected, to be sure, of explaining how principles could be "self-evident" when there were obviously so many people who did not believe them. Circumstance nearly solved this problem for the Americans, giving them, as it were, a national exemption from Hume's attack on natural law—which may be one of the reasons why they almost invariably ignored it. When one's ultimate values are accepted wherever one turns, the absolute language of self-evidence comes easily enough.

This then is the mood of America's absolutism: the sober faith that its norms are self-evident. It is one of the most powerful absolutisms in the world, more powerful even than the messianic spirit of the Continental liberals which, as we saw, the Americans were able to reject. That spirit arose out of contact with an opposing way of life, and its very intensity betrayed an inescapable element of doubt. But the American absolutism, flowing from an honest experience with universality, lacked even the passion that doubt might give. It was so sure of itself that it hardly needed to become articulate, so secure that it could actually support a pragmatism which seemed on the surface to belie it. American pragmatism has always been deceptive because, glacier-like, it has rested on miles of submerged conviction, and the conformitarian ethos which that conviction generates has always been infuriating because it has refused to pay its critics the compliment of an argument. . . .

When we study national variations in political theory, we are led to semantic considerations of a delicate kind, and it is to these, finally, that we must turn if we wish to get at the basic assumption of American thought. We have to consider the peculiar meaning that American life gave to the words of Locke.

There are two sides to the Lockean argument: a defense of the state that is implicit, and a limitation of the state that is explicit. The first is to be found in Locke's basic social norm, the concept of free individuals in a state of nature. This idea untangled men from the myriad associations of class, church, guild, and place, in terms of which feudal society defined their lives; and by doing so, it automatically gave to the state a much higher rank in relation to them than ever before. The state became

the only association that might legitimately coerce them at all. That is why the liberals of France in the eighteenth century were able to substitute the concept of absolutism for Locke's conclusions of limited government and to believe that they were still his disciples in the deepest sense. When Locke came to America, however, a change appeared. Because the basic feudal oppressions of Europe had not taken root, the fundamental social norm of Locke ceased in large part to look like a norm and began, of all things, to look like a sober description of fact. The effect was significant enough. When the Americans moved from that concept to the contractual idea of organizing the state, they were not conscious of having already done anything to fortify the state, but were conscious only that they were about to limit it. One side of Locke became virtually the whole of him. . . .

It was a remarkable thing—this inversion of perspectives that made the social norms of Europe the factual premises of America. History was on a lark, out to tease men, not by shattering their dreams, but by fulfilling them with a sort of satiric accuracy. In America one not only found a society sufficiently fluid to give a touch of meaning to the individualist norms of Locke, but one also found letter-perfect replicas of the very images he used. There was a frontier that was a veritable state of nature. There were agreements, such as the Mayflower Compact, that were veritable social contracts. There were new communities springing up *in vacuis locis,* clear evidence that men were using their Lockean right of emigration, which Jefferson soberly appealed to as "universal" in his defense of colonial land claims in 1774. A purist could argue, of course, that even these phenomena were not enough to make a reality out of the presocial men that liberalism dreamt of in theory. But surely they came as close to doing so as anything history has ever seen. Locke and Rousseau themselves could not help lapsing into the empirical mood when they looked across the Atlantic. "Thus, in the beginning," Locke once wrote, "all the world was America. . . ."

In such a setting, how could the tremendous, revolutionary social impact that liberalism had in Europe be preserved? The impact was not, of course, missing entirely; for the attack on the vestiges of corporate society in America that began in 1776, the disestablishment of the Anglican church, the abolition of quitrents and primogeniture, the breaking up of the Tory estates, tinged American liberalism with its own peculiar fire.[2] Nor must we therefore assume that the Americans had wider political objectives than the Europeans, since even their new governmental forms were, as Becker once said, little more than the "colonial institutions with the Parliament and king left out" But after these cautions have been taken, the central point is clear. In America the first half of Locke's argument was bound to become less a call to arms than a set of preliminary remarks essential to establishing a final conclusion: that the power of the state must be limited. Observe how it is treated by the Americans in their great debate with England, even by original thinkers like Otis and Wilson. They do not lavish upon it the fascinated inquiry that we find in Rousseau or Priestley. They advance it mechanically, hurry through it, anxious to

get on to what is really bothering them: the limits of the British Parliament, the power of taxation. In Europe the idea of social liberty is loaded with dynamite; but in America it becomes, to a remarkable degree, the working base from which argument begins.

Here, then, is the master assumption of American political thought, the assumption from which all of the American attitudes discussed in this essay flow: the reality of atomistic social freedom. It is instinctive to the American mind, as in a sense the concept of the polis was instinctive to Platonic Athens or the concept of the church to the mind of the middle ages. . . .

It might be appropriate to summarize with a single word, or even with a single sentence, the political outlook that this premise has produced. But where is the word and where is the sentence one might use? American political thought, as we have seen, is a veritable maze of polar contradictions, winding in and out of each other hopelessly: pragmatism and absolutism, historicism and rationalism, optimism and pessimism, materialism and idealism, individualism and conformism. But, after all, the human mind works by polar contradictions; and when we have evolved an interpretation of it which leads cleanly in a single direction, we may be sure that we have missed a lot. The task of the cultural analyst is not to discover simplicity, or even to discover unity, for simplicity and unity do not exist, but to drive a wedge of rationality through the pathetic indecisions of social thought. In the American case that wedge is not hard to find. It is not hidden in an obscure place. We find it in what the West as a whole has always recognized to be the distinctive element in American civilization: its social freedom, its social equality. And yet it is true, for all of our Jeffersonian nationalism, that the interpretation of American political

---

[2] The distinctive nature of these reforms is that they were a fulfillment of the past rather than, as in Europe, a revolt against it. The elimination of feudal vestiges in a society already under the dominion of liberalism is an entirely different matter from the introduction of liberalism in a society still heavily ridden by feudal forms. America's "social revolution" thus is not to be compared with the great social revolutions of Europe. I am reserving this general problem for another discussion.

thought has not been built around this idea. On the contrary, instead of interpreting the American revolution in terms of American freedom, we have interpreted it in terms of American oppression. . . . We have missed what the rest of the world has seen and what we ourselves have seen whenever we have contrasted the New World with the Old. . . .

The liberals of Europe in 1776 were obviously worshipping a very peculiar hero. If the average American had been suddenly thrust in their midst, he would have been embarrassed by the millennial enthusiasms that many of them had, would have found their talk of classes vastly overdone, and would have reacted to the Enlightenment synthesis of absolutism and liberty as if it were little short of dishonest doubletalk. Bred in a freer world, he had a different set of perspectives, was animated by a different set of passions, and looked forward to different goals. He was, as Crèvecoeur put it, a "new man" in Western politics.

But, someone will ask, where did the liberal heritage of the Americans come from in the first place? Didn't they have to create it? And if they did, were they not at one time or another in much the same position as the Europeans?

These questions drive us back to the ultimate nature of the American experience, and, doing so, confront us with a queer twist in the problem of revolution. No one can deny that conscious purpose went into the making of the colonial world, and that the men of the seventeenth century who fled to America from Europe were keenly aware of the oppressions of European life. But they were revolutionaries with a difference, and the fact of their fleeing is no minor fact: for it is one thing to stay at home and fight the "canon and feudal law," and it is another to leave it far behind. It is one thing to try to establish lib-

eralism in the Old World, and it is another to establish it in the New. Revolution, to borrow the words of T. S. Eliot, means to murder and create, but the American experience has been projected strangely in the realm of creation alone. The destruction of forests and Indian tribes—heroic, bloody, legendary as it was—cannot be compared with the destruction of a social order to which one belongs oneself. The first experience is wholly external and, being external, can actually be completed; the second experience is an inner struggle as well as an outer struggle, like the slaying of a Freudian father, and goes on in a sense forever. Moreover, even the matter of creation is not in the American case a simple one. The New World, as Lord Baltimore's ill-fated experiment with feudalism in the seventeenth century illustrates, did not merely offer the Americans a virgin ground for the building of a liberal system: it conspired itself to help that system along. The abundance of land in America, as well as the need for a lure to settlers, entered so subtly into the shaping of America's liberal tradition, touched it so completely at every point, that Sumner was actually ready to say, "We have not made America, America has made us."

It is this business of destruction and creation which goes to the heart of the problem. For the point of departure of great revolutionary thought everywhere else in the world has been the effort to build a new society on the ruins of an old society, and this is an experience America has never had. Tocqueville saw the issue clearly, and it is time now to complete the sentence of his with which we began this essay: "The great advantage of the American is that he has arrived at a state of democracy without having to endure a democratic revolution; *and that he is born free without having to become so.*"

In contrast with Louis Hartz, ELISHA P. DOUGLASS (b. 1915) finds genuine conflict among the revolutionary generation. Within the several states, he claims, there developed very real contests for political power, conflicts that reflected meaningfully different views of what the social and political order ought to be. What does Douglass' essay suggest about the relationship between ideology and its social and political context? Douglass raises as well the point that revolutionary movements have a way of splitting apart once the common external enemy is removed. Why is this so? Douglass teaches American history at the University of North Carolina.*

Elisha P. Douglass

Ideological Conflicts:
Whigs Versus Democrats

In recent years there has been considerable speculation about the causes of the American Revolution, but less, perhaps, about its essential characteristics. Was it primarily radical, a break from tradition which separated the destiny of America from that of Europe and ultimately produced a unique American character, or was it conservative, a reorientation of colonial and European experience to meet the needs of independence? Was the Revolution the result of a spontaneous upsurge of idealism seeking political and institutional expression, or was it a simple struggle over who, rather than what, should rule? Or if all these diverse elements were present, what were their proportions in the composition of the whole?

There are no simple answers to these questions because modern revolutions are complex and not simple phenomena. When any substantial portion of a population rises against lawful authority, its own internal conflicts are only temporarily shelved in the pursuit of a common objective. The various groups throwing their weight against existing government usually have different plans for the future; only the commonly shared oppression induces them to subordinate individual objectives for the main task at hand. But once the oppressor has been removed, group aims again become paramount. The chief cause of disagreement is usually the amount of change to be effected by the revolt. It suddenly becomes apparent that what were

*From Elisha P. Douglass, *Rebels and Democrats* (Chapel Hill, N.C.: University of North Carolina Press, 1955), pp. 1–8, 13–32. Footnotes omitted.

ends for one group are only means for another. Thus revolutionists naturally fall into classifications of conservative and radical. The simplicity of the revolutionary movement dissolves into the complexity inherent in the normal course of politics.

The American Revolution is no exception to the rule, but its complexity is not so apparent as that of many other revolutions, for its characteristics were predominantly conservative, as some students of the period have noted. Yet it had a less conspicuous but important radical aspect. In many ways it represented the culmination of a desire for the abolition of political privilege on the part of groups outside the politically active classes who felt that in the past they had not received the consideration they deserved.

This desire for political reform did not suddenly come into being with the suppression of British authority. From the first days of settlement it had been a factor—although often a minor one—in the periodic outbreaks of violence directed against governors and royal officials. The gentlemen and the corporations who founded the first settlements, whether for profit or the glory of God, had all tried to reproduce the social system of England with only such variations as suited their special purposes. Such men as Penn and Calvert saw no incompatibility between applied philanthropy and a hierarchical society headed by themselves. The lords spiritual of Massachusetts had no intention of translating the equality of all men before God into equality in civil society. The gentlemen who headed the Virginia Company and the Carolina Proprietors subordinated any desires for self-expression on the part of their settlers to the primary object of profit and prestige for themselves. Yet in almost every instance the carefully laid plans of the founders were frustrated by the failure of the settlers to cooperate and

by the natural conditions of America. Once possessed of freeholds, the former tenant farmers of England exhibited a tendency to demand commensurate political privileges; a degree of economic independence promoted a desire to be consulted in the political process. . . .

The sometimes hostile and uncooperative attitude of the settlers toward their governments was usually not motivated by a conscious desire for more democracy, although this may sometimes have been a factor. It would be a mistake to read into the tumultuous history of seventeenth-century America any continuing trend of class or sectional struggle. Usually specific grievances like the lack of protection from the government against Indians, unfair land distribution, high taxes, lack of a circulating medium, and extortion by officials were the cause of uprisings. The ease of acquiring land (except in New York), the wide dispersal of the population, the lack of communications, the remnants of a tradition of subordination, and the relative lack of class distinctions all conspired to retard the growth of conscious radicalism.

Yet in most of the periodic outbreaks against constituted authority there can be detected a thread of resentment against the few who had political privilege. Toward the end of the seventeenth century white servitude and the utilization of slave labor in the South, the expanding commercial activities in the northern towns, and the tremendous profits gained by privileged land speculation widened the gap between rich and poor. The raising of property qualifications for voting and office-holding, the close hold of the aristocracy on local government, and the under-representation of frontier districts gradually changed the assemblies from bodies truly representative of the people to political organs of the upper classes. This rise of a native aristocracy to a commanding position in politics apparently gave impetus to the occasional half-felt desire for the equalization of rights on the part of groups among the lower classes. The Land Bank incident in Massachusetts, the Paxton Riots of Pennsylvania, the "Great Rebellion of 1766" in New York, and the Regulator War in North Carolina all gave expression to a protest against privilege. On the eve of the Revolution, the dissatisfaction which had resulted in these outbreaks formed small but nourishing culture beds for the growth of democracy.

The appeals for freedom voiced by colonial leaders during the early years of the Revolution, the loosening of restraints which followed the suppression of British authority, and the necessity of redefining the relations of rulers and ruled in the succession governments all gave inspiration and opportunity for the transformation of latent resentment, where it existed, into a demand for political democracy. This development provoked immediate opposition from the Revolutionary leaders, for most of them were basically conservative and felt that majority rule and political equality constituted not only a threat to their dominant political position but a danger to the very freedoms for which the struggle against Britain had been undertaken. Circumstances divided the Revolutionary leaders into well-defined radical and moderate groupings regarding the separation from Britain; Whigs in colonies where assemblies had been dissolved and military operations were underway were usually more eager for separation than members of their party in colonies where reconciliation could be effected more easily. But in their ideas regarding the institutions and relationships to be included in the succession governments the Revolutionary leaders showed a rather surprising uniformity. All were agreed that the primary purpose of government was to protect rights and that

the strongest possible barriers should be erected against the arbitrary use of power but they did not conclude that the best way to effect these objectives was to place all power in the hands of the people. Far from it; as men of their age they feared that unchecked majorities of constituents or representatives would be as productive of tyranny as an unchecked despot.

In addition to these weighty considerations, the economic and political interests of the Revolutionary leaders led them to oppose democracy. Many of these men, particularly in the South, came from the high aristocracy and all were quite a social cut above the masses of the people. Possessing both property and power, they had much to lose and nothing to gain from a democratic reform of colonial institutions. Hence it is understandable that they resisted the attempts made by groups whose interests often conflicted with their own to seize the operative sovereignty in the state governments. In common with the possessors of wealth and power of every age, they considered the maintenance of their privileges to be an integral part of any political organization established in the name of liberty.

The Revolutionary leaders, therefore, were presented with two basic problems at the outset of the Revolution—the protection of rights against the arbitrary use of power, and the maintenance of their own superior position in the new state governments. The obvious solution was to establish constitutions which would include as many of the safeguards as possible utilized in colonial government. A revival of any semblance of the prerogative power was of course out of the question, but property qualifications for voting and officeholding and the principle of bicameralism had not been discredited by identification with British tyranny. These defenses against mobs and despots had been sanctioned by colonial experience and had become an integral part of the provincial governments; prudence dictated that they be included in the new state governments.

A political science devoted in part to frustrating majority will might at first glance seem inconsistent with the political philosophy of the Revolutionary leaders. From a modern point of view property qualifications seem incompatible with the doctrine of government by consent; the popular sovereignty emblazoned upon the Declaration of Independence appears in some measure to be qualified by the checks and balances of the first state constitutions. The men of '76 did not feel any conflict between their guiding principles and their political practice, however, because their principles contained many conservative assumptions which are often overlooked today. The rights they proclaimed were what they believed to be the traditional rights of Englishmen, not new and unprecedented privileges. The vocabulary of natural rights used in the Declaration of Independence did not indicate a sudden change to a more radical philosophy but was rather, as Carl Becker has indicated, an attempt to rephrase English rights in such a way that they would appeal to contemporary European intellectuals. The assertion of equality was not intended as a protest against the social distinctions, political privilege, and unequal distribution of wealth in the colonies but was rather a repudiation of hereditary status and the privilege derived from it in Britain and on the Continent. The assertion of the right of revolution, apart from its actual consequences, can scarcely be called a radical gesture in view of Locke's endorsement and the general acceptance of the proposition by previous generations of Englishmen. No one doubted the right of revolution; the only question was whether circumstances justified its invocation. In-

dependence was for most of the Revolutionists a desperate measure of last resort. In their own minds they were defending the body of traditional English rights against an omnipotent, and therefore revolutionary, Parliament. Not accepting the Parliamentary supremacy implicit in the eighteenth-century British constitution, they considered themselves as counterrevolutionists rather than as rebels against lawful authority.

Any apparent discrepancies between the political philosophy and the political science of the Revolutionary leaders are therefore to a large extent reconciled by a pervasive conservatism which underlay the whole Revolutionary movement. The Whig leaders of 1776 could congratulate themselves after the struggle that their revolution, like that of 1688, was glorious as much for what it left untouched as for what it had altered. The traditional British institutions inherited from the empire had been remoulded into republican forms, traditional British rights were guaranteed to all American citizens, in most states the original leaders of the revolutionary party were firmly in control of the succession governments, and despite occasional shocks the colonial social system had weathered the levelling tendencies of the conflict.

Yet these felicitous results were not reached without occasional sharp conflicts with the less privileged groups among the rank and file who wanted to lower the center of gravity of political power. Both Whig and democrat were equally dedicated to the maintenance of human rights, both were equally opposed to arbitrary rule, but agreement on the fundamental postulates of a liberal philosophy could not settle the conflict over the location of political power. Thus the Revolution in some states acquired a dual nature. On one hand it was an uprising against British authority, on the other a movement for the democratic reform of all the institutions of provincial government whether tainted by the British connection or not. It would be a mistake, however, to assume from these instances that social upheaval was imminent throughout the country in 1776. As previously indicated, democratic agitation, although bitter and insistent, was localized, temporary, and unorganized. For the most part, the politically unprivileged came loyally to the support of the Revolutionary leadership and provided the sinews of the Continental armies. . . .

It was Thomas Paine who first identified the Revolution with democracy. The only Whig propagandist who was not a member of the colonial ruling class, neither merchant, lawyer, nor planter, Paine spoke in the language of the common people. *Common Sense* was a breath of fresh air to a propaganda literature which was beginning to suffocate on legalisms. The educated might be impressed by Dickinson's and Dulany's briefs for an equitable division of taxing power between colonies and mother country and by Jefferson's and Wilson's theory that the alleged expatriation of the colonists justified their claim for autonomy, but argument on this level could have little meaning for the man on the street or at the plow. Everyone, however, could understand Paine's contention that America was an independent continent temporarily held in subjection by a vicious despot who derived his authority from a no less vicious system of government.

Paine conceived the Revolution as the means of establishing a new society based on equal rights. The struggle would be the symbolic labor pains attending the birth of a new order which would realize the heritage of freedom withheld for countless generations. "We have it in our power to begin the world over again," he announced. "The birthday of a new world is

at hand, and a race of men, perhaps as numerous as all Europe contains, are to receive their portion of freedom from the events of a few months. Every spot in the old world is overrun with oppression. Freedom hath been hunted round the globe. Asia and Africa have long expelled her. Europe regards her like a stranger, and England hath given her warning to depart. O! receive the fugitive and prepare in time an asylum for mankind."

This strain of utopianism, this vision of a better world as the object of the Revolution, is stronger in Paine than in any of his contemporaries. Once the prerogative power had been suppressed and the royal officialdom overthrown, most of the Revolutionary leaders were quite content to see a continuation of existing social and political relationships. For them the internal revolution was concluded by the summer of 1776. The task remaining was to insure the stability of society on its present basis; hence they turned for guidance in matters of government to colonial experience and to authorities who had already proved to be sound, such as Milton, Sidney, Bolingbroke, and Montesquieu. But Paine's conception of an adequate governmental framework owed nothing to authority or tradition. It represented only the minimum amount of machinery necessary to translate the will of majorities into legislation and insure unity among the colonies— unicameral assemblies in the states based on proportionate representation and subject to the Continental Congress.

An anonymous Massachusetts pamphleteer who wrote about the same time and whose ideas were reflected later among democrats during constitutional struggles in that state, was more openly critical of the plans of government supported by the Revolutionary leaders. Asserting that the people "best know their wants and necessities and therefore are best able to govern themselves," he condemned upper houses armed with a veto and not directly responsible to the electorate as unworthy of a free state and declared that advocates of this type of bicameralism had designs against liberty. "The people are now contending for freedom; and would to God they might not only obtain, but likewise keep it in their own hands. There are many very noisy about liberty but are aiming at nothing more than personal power and grandeur. And are not many, under the delusive character of guardians of their country, collecting influence and honor only for oppression?" He felt that representation should be in proportion to population, and that all adult free males should have the suffrage. Property qualifications for office he regarded as a source of corruption. "Social virtue and knowledge . . . is the best and only necessary qualification of [a representative]. So sure as we make interest necessary in this case, as sure we root out virtue. . . . The notion of an estate has the directest tendency to set up the avarisious [sic] over the heads of the poor. . . . Let it not be said in future generations that money was made by the founders of the American states an essential qualification in the rulers of a free people." By his plan of government the executive and the judges would be selected by annual elections and the executive denied a veto. In a unique provision he stipulated that an appeal from superior court decisions would lie to the House of Representatives. "The judges, in many cases, are obliged . . . to put such a construction on matters as they think most agreeable to the spirit and reason of the law. Now so far as they are reduced to this necessity, they assume what is in fact the prerogative of the legislature, for those that made the laws ought to give them a meaning when they are doubtful." . . .

Common Sense and *The People the Best Governors* together illustrate the aspirations for a better world and the desire to equalize political rights which characterized the democratic groups in the Revolution. For them the preamble of the Declaration of Independence was more than a collection of philosophical postulates; it was a set of principles to be incorporated into political institutions. Popular sovereignty and equality were to be realized by manhood suffrage, the abolition of property qualifications for officeholding, representation according to population, and a government directly responsible in all its branches to the people as a whole.

The Whig leaders in the spring of 1776 were not slow to realize the threat to the established order in the confusion accompanying the Revolution. Wrote Paine, "I have heard some men say . . . that they dreaded an independence, fearing that it would produce civil wars: . . . " John Adams was one of these. "From the beginning, " he declared, "I always expected we should have more difficulty and danger in our attempts to govern ourselves and in our negotiations and connections with foreign powers than from all the fleets and armies of Great Britain." His kinsman, Sam Adams, found in 1776 that many Whig leaders felt the establishment of new governments would serve as a cloak for licentiousness. Thus many representatives from colonies not already committed to war by the turn of events became almost desperate in their attempts to bring about a reconciliation with Britain.

Before the suppression of royal government brought confusion to the colonies many Whigs had belittled the dangers to be anticipated from mob violence—at least in public. . . .

But by 1776 the tolerant Whig attitude toward lawlessness underwent a transformation. The responsibilities of government gave them a new appreciation of the necessity for order, authority, and subordination. The rascals had been turned out; therefore good patriots should settle down and show a proper respect for authority. "How much soever I may heretofore have found fault with the powers that were I suppose I shall be well pleased now to hear submission inculcated to the powers that are," wrote John Adams. Elbridge Gerry complained from Massachusetts that the people were feeling too strongly their new importance and needed a curb, and James Warren, speaker of the Massachusetts House, dreaded the consequences of "the leveling spirit, encouraged and drove to such lengths as it is." Sam Adams, to whom *vox populi* had been *vox Dei* when Hutchinson was in office, felt that there was "danger of errors on the side of the people" after the Whig leaders had seized control in Massachusetts. James Allen, a Pennsylvania Whig and a member of a wealthy family which had been a constant recipient of the proprietors' patronage, retired to his country seat in 1776 because the "mobility is triumphant." . . .

When the course of events in the various colonies made it clear that there was no middle ground between capitulation to British demands and independence, the radical section of the Whig party firmly, if with misgivings, moved to seize the sovereign power. Thus Massachusetts established government under the provincial charter in order, among other things, to counter "the alarming symptoms of the abatement in the minds of the people of the sacredness of private property." Edmund Pendleton, accepting the presidency of the Virginia Convention, observed, "It will become us to reflect whether we can longer sustain the great struggle we are making in this situation." In Pennsylvania, many of the radical Whigs who had in 1774 done their best to discredit the pro-prietary government rallied to its support when the threat of internal revolution appeared imminent.

Lack of plans and procedures for the formation of succession governments as well as the gravity of seizing the sovereignty embarrassed the Whig leaders. Although *Common Sense* had received enthusiastic approval from radicals because of its castigation of Britain, its suggestions on government elicited at best silence and at worst active opposition. Conservatives denounced the pamphlet in unmeasured terms. Landon Carter, a Virginia planter, could hardly restrain his rage. *Common Sense,* he asserted, was "repleat with art and contradiction . . . rascally and nonsensical . . . a sophisticated attempt to throw all men out of Principles . . . which has drove all who espouse it from the justice of their contest." . . .

One of the most important effects of *Common Sense* was that in large part it stirred John Adams to write his famous *Thoughts on Government,* a pamphlet of almost equal importance in American history. Whereas *Common Sense* was the inspiration for independence and a new equalitarian society, *Thoughts on Government* erected the framework of American republicanism out of the solid materials of traditional institutions. The two stand as symbols of the democratic and conservative programs, the thesis and antithesis of the Revolution. Tom Paine, devastating as he was in his attack on hereditary government, had little of a practical nature to put in its place. Adams could never have matched Paine's fire and common sense logic in presenting the case for independence, but his intellectual background made him much more able to construct a stable and practical government which would appeal to the ruling class. . . .

In his autobiography . . . written many years after the event—Adams claimed that he wrote the pamphlet to counteract the pernicious influence of Paine's political ideas. He "dreaded the effect so popular a pamphlet might have among the people, and determined to do all in his power to counteract the effect of it.". . .

Although Adams' account in later life exaggerates his antipathy for Paine in 1776, it is nevertheless clear that an important object of *Thoughts on Government* was to correct what he regarded as the dangerous heresies to be found in *Common Sense.*

The central theme of Adams' political architecture was the separation of powers, a device which he thought would check the drift toward social revolution. Since the separation of powers has had such a tremendous influence on American political thought and has been such a mainstay of conservatism, it will be necessary to examine its assumptions, processes, and objectives.

Like Locke's theory of compact and natural law, separation of powers was a very old idea, even in the eighteenth century. It was discussed by Aristotle and was perhaps even known to Herodotus. It may be defined as a political device designed to maintain stability in constitutional government by so balancing governmental organs and functions that power-seeking individuals and groups would automatically check each other before they could endanger the state. If democracy has always rested on an assumption that man is essentially cooperative, the theory of separation of powers in the eighteenth century was based on the premise that man is essentially unsocial, devoted exclusively to his own interests, and prepared to make war on his fellows at any time when advantage outweighed risk. According to the theory, government should not try to repress disruptive forces, for if it was strong enough to accomplish this it would be an oppressive force in itself. Rather it should direct these

forces in such a way that they would neutralize each other. Like the balance of power in international affairs, the separation of powers was considered the only way to maintain stability and the moral order in an essentially unstable and immoral world.

There were three conceptions, or variants, of separation of powers in the eighteenth century. The first, and most primitive, was "balanced government" or "mixed monarchy." By this interpretation the medieval estates of the realm—crown, clergy, nobles, and commons—symbolized and represented the principal classes in society, and a balanced government kept them in equilibrium. Each estate was identified with a certain form of government— the king, monarchy; the nobles, aristocracy; the people, democracy. Each form had certain advantages and disadvantages. When it stood alone as a "simple" government, the disadvantages—or "weaknesses," as contemporary theorists preferred to call them—were greater than the advantages; but when the three forms were mixed together as in the British constitution, the disadvantages cancelled each other out by some mysterious metaphysical process never explained but never doubted. The second conception of separation of powers was the separation of the organs or departments of government. This interpretation was partially a functional abstraction of balanced government and partially an attempt empirically to analyse the processes of government as a whole. Prior to 1776 colonial leaders thought of the separation of powers as mixed monarchy; when monarchical institutions became discredited they viewed crown, nobles, and commons functionally as executive, senate, and house of representatives. The third conception of the separation of powers was the equal distribution of the multitude of political functions performed by any government. This view predominated in the Federal Convention of 1787. Nomination, veto, appropriation, impeachment, trial of impeachment, judgment, treaty making, and the like were assigned to the different departments in such a way that each department would have equal weight. This was the most effective application of separation of powers, for only the proper distribution of functions could give the balance which was the object of separation. Separation without the balance of power would be of little help in maintaining stability.

The separation of powers derives its essential character from the type of institutions it is designed to protect. Applied to a democratic government it brings stability and efficiency without loss of responsiveness to the people, but applied to the essentially hierarchical institutions of the eighteenth century it became a means of blocking popular expression and insuring the continuance of classified citizenship. Both the democrats and the conservatives of the Revolution, appreciating its value, included it in their programs, but in somewhat different forms and with quite different objectives. Democrats, viewing it primarily as a safeguard against a monopoly of political power by the upper classes, made it the basis of their demands for the abolition of plural office holdings; conservatives, conceiving it as a safeguard against arbitrary rule by mob or despot, gave it institutional expression in their plans for bicameral legislatures.

It is entirely understandable, therefore, that Adams, in combating what he felt to be the drift toward social revolution, should seize on the separation of powers institutionalized in bicameralism as the best hope for maintaining stability, human rights, and the leadership of the Whig revolutionaries in the succession governments. And in so doing he made Montesquieu, not Locke, the chief luminary among political philosophers, for Montesquieu had conceived—wrongly, of course—that separation of powers was the guiding principle of the eighteenth-century British constitution and the only way to avert tyranny from either mob or despot. With the Revolutionary congresses, conventions, and committees in mind, Adams declared that single assemblies were capricious, avaricious, and ambitious. They "would make arbitrary laws for their own interest, execute all laws arbitrarily for their own interest, and adjudge all controversies in their own favor." In order to secure stability and the rule of justice, therefore, Adams would create a second house, independent alike of the people and their representatives, to act as a check upon the lower. The executive power he would place in the hands of a governor assisted by a council, and, as a further check upon the legislature, he suggested for the executive an absolute veto. In later writings Adams treated the two houses as representative of the democratic and aristocratic elements in society. They would be perpetually in conflict, he felt; a victory of either would bring despotism. Therefore the governor occupied a key position in maintaining a balance. In this tripartite system Adams recreated the elements of mixed monarchy in the form of a "regal republic."

If the common people were to have only a one-third interest in government under the Adams scheme, the lower house at least was to be their very own. "It should be in miniature an exact portrait of the people at large. It should think, feel, reason, and act like them." But Adams did not implement this logic by advocating manhood suffrage for the lower house. Instead he called on the states "to agree on the number and qualifications of persons who shall have the benefit of choosing . . . representatives." In his view, the propertyless should be classified with women and children as inherently unfit to vote. "Is it not true," he wrote to James Sullivan, "that men in general, in every society, who are wholly destitute of property, are also too little acquainted with public affairs to form a right judgment and too dependent on other men to have a will of their own? If this is a fact, if you give to every man who has no property a vote, will you not make a fine encouraging provision for corruption by your fundamental law? Such is the frailty of the human heart that very few men who have no property have any judgment of their own."

Adams' fear of manhood suffrage was based primarily on English rather than American experience. In Parliamentary elections, tenant farmers had proved to be very susceptible to bribery and corruption, primarily because they did not have the economic security to afford independent judgment. Therefore eighteenth-century conservatives perhaps had some justification for fearing that if the suffrage were broadened under similar circumstances, impecunious voters might become the willing tools of demagogues. Quite possibly infatuated majorities might demand a redistribution of wealth or an overthrow of the constitution. . . .

Forecasts of the consequences of manhood suffrage and the abolition of property qualifications for office varied. Some conservatives . . . were particularly anxious for the safety of property. Others—like Adams—while not ignoring this threat felt that the danger of dictatorship and the loss of constitutional liberties was greater. But few, if any, of the Whig leaders evidenced any awareness of the basic contradiction between a limited suffrage and their equalitarian philosophy. Hence a double paradox: to preserve their own liberty, the unprivileged masses must be prevented from infringing on the privileged few; to maintain a government based on consent, a large proportion of the people must be deprived of the ability to extend or withhold consent.

The effect of Adams' pamphlet, *Thoughts on Government,* can hardly be overestimated. Most Whig leaders, although worried by the growing anarchy and disregard for private property exhibited by their more humble followers, had not yet realized that permanent stability could be reached only by abolishing the dictatorship of the Revolutionary congresses and committees. Regarding royal governors and councils as the greatest threat to freedom, they were determined above all else to avoid a re-establishment of anything which resembled the prerogative. So strong was the obsessive fear of executive power that even in 1787 it constituted the greatest obstacle which the Federalists had to face in their drive for a balanced government. But if Adams could not persuade the Whig leaders to establish strong governors, he at least convinced them of the need for bicameral legislatures. Only Pennsylvania, Georgia and Vermont stubbornly adhered to democratic unicameralism. *Thoughts on Government* was not only discussed in the committee drafting the North Carolina constitution but was written verbatim into the executive letter book. Arriving in Virginia at the moment the constitution was under discussion, it was enthusiastically received by Patrick Henry. Jonathan Dickinson Sergeant adopted some of its provisions for the constitution of New Jersey, and—according to Adams—the constitution of New York was modelled on his plan. Finally, he was able literally to translate *Thoughts on Government* into political reality when he drafted the Massachusetts Constitution of 1780. Thus in five states his proposals were possibly the paramount guide in composing the first instruments of government, and, when it is considered that the state constitutions—particularly that of Massachusetts—were the greatest single influence on the Federal Constitution, the full importance of the pamphlet should be evident. In the words of one authority, "Adams' ideas, more than those of any other single person, guided and pervaded the movement which established republican government in America, and therefore in the modern world."

Common Sense, The People the Best Governors, and *Thoughts on Government* made clear in 1776 what the issues were to be in the forthcoming struggle between democrats and conservatives to write their political ideas into the first state constitutions. Al-though the necessity for compromise made both groups relinquish their extreme demands, the democratic ideal continued to be a simple government with a sovereign legislature—preferably unicameral—directly dependent upon an electorate which included all adult, free males. In contrast to this equalitarianism, the Revolutionary leaders were to press for complex governments based on the separation of powers and traditional institutions which would preserve the existing social system, guard the existing distribution of wealth, preserve human rights, and secure the dominance of the Revolutionary party in the new regimes.

Most scholars who have compared the American with European revolutions have concluded that the American experience was much less intense, indeed was scarcely revolutionary at all in its results. R. R. PALMER (b. 1909), professor of modern European history at Yale, argues the opposite. In portions of his *Age of the Democratic Revolution* not included here, he affirms that both socially and politically the American Revolution was fully as disruptive as the French. As evidence he cites the number of exiles per capita and the amounts of redistributed property for the two nations. On the level of political ideology, his findings are somewhat less clear. From the essay that follows, does one conclude that America's revolutionary ideology was radical? Or was the act of founding governments based on what was actually a familiar and rather moderate set of beliefs?*

R. R. Palmer

The People as Constituent Power

If it be asked what the American Revolution distinctively contributed to the world's stock of ideas, the answer might go somewhat along these lines. It did not contribute primarily a social doctrine—for although a certain skepticism toward social rank was an old American attitude, and possibly even a gift to mankind, it long antedated the Revolution, which did not so much cut down, as prevent the growth of, an aristocracy of European type. It did not especially contribute economic ideas—for the Revolution had nothing to teach on the production or distribution of goods, and the most advanced parties objected to private wealth only when it became too closely associated with government. They aimed at a separation of economic and political spheres, by which men of wealth, while free to get rich, should not have a disproportionate influence on government, and, on the other hand, government and public emoluments should not be used as a means of livelihood for an otherwise impecunious and unproductive upper class.

The American Revolution was a political movement, concerned with liberty, and with power. Most of the ideas involved were by no means distinctively American. There was nothing peculiarly American in the concepts, purely as concepts, of natural liberty and equality. They were admitted by conservatives, and were taught in the theological faculty at the Sorbonne. Nor could Americans claim any exclusive understanding of the ideas of government by

*From R. R. Palmer, *The Age of the Democratic Revolution* (Princeton, N.J.: Princeton University Press, 1959–1964), vol. 1, pp. 213–217, 221–228, 232–235. Reprinted by permission of Princeton University Press, and Oxford University Press. Footnotes omitted.

contract or consent, or the sovereignty of the people, or political representation, or the desirability of independence from foreign rule, or natural rights, or the difference between natural law and positive law, or between certain fundamental laws and ordinary legislation, or the separation of powers, or the federal union of separate states. All these ideas were perfectly familiar in Europe, and that is why the American Revolution was of such interest to Europeans.

The most distinctive work of the Revolution was in finding a method, and furnishing a model, for putting these ideas into practical effect. It was in the implementation of similar ideas that Americans were more successful than Europeans. "In the last fifty years," wrote General Bonaparte to Citizen Talleyrand in 1797, "there is only one thing that I can see that we have really defined, and that is the sovereignty of the people. But we have had no more success in determining what is constitutional, than in allocating the different powers of government." And he said more peremptorily, on becoming Emperor in 1804, that the time had come "to constitute the Nation." He added: "I am the constituent power."

The problem throughout much of America and Europe, for half a century, was to "constitute" new government, and in a measure new societies. The problem was to find a constituent power. Napoleon offered himself to Europe in this guise. The Americans solved the problem by the device of the constitutional convention, which, revolutionary in origin, soon became institutionalized in the public law of the United States.

The constitutional convention in theory embodied the sovereignty of the people. The people chose it for a specific purpose, not to govern, but to set up institutions of government. The convention, acting as the sovereign people, proceeded to draft a constitution and a declaration of rights. Certain "natural" or "inalienable" rights of the citizen were thus laid down at the same time as the powers of government. It was the constitution that created the powers of government, defined their scope, gave them legality, and balanced them one against another. The constitution was written and comprised in a single document. The constitution and accompanying declaration, drafted by the convention, must, in the developed theory, be ratified by the people. The convention thereupon disbanded and disappeared, lest its members have a vested interest in the offices they created. The constituent power went into abeyance, leaving the work of government to the authorities now constituted. The people, having exercised sovereignty, now came under government. Having made law, they came under law. They put themselves voluntarily under restraint. At the same time, they put restraint upon government. All government was limited government; all public authority must keep within the bounds of the constitution and of the declared rights. There were two levels of law, a higher law or constitution that only the people could make or amend, through constitutional conventions or bodies similarly empowered; and a statutory law, to be made and unmade, within the assigned limits, by legislators to whom the constitution gave this function.

Such was the theory, and it was a distinctively American one. European thinkers, in all their discussion of a political or social contract, of government by consent and of sovereignty of the people, had not clearly imagined the people as actually contriving a constitution and creating the organs of government. They lacked the idea of the people as a constituent power. Even in the French Revolution the idea developed slowly; members of the French

National Assembly, long after the Tennis Court oath, continued to feel that the constitution which they were writing, to be valid, had to be accepted by the King as a kind of equal with whom the nation had to negotiate. Nor, indeed, would the King tolerate any other view. . . .

The difficulty with the theory was that the conditions under which it could work were seldom present. No people really starts *de novo;* some political institutions always already exist; there is never a *tabula rasa,* or state of nature, or Chart Blanche as Galloway posited for conservative purposes. Also, it is difficult for a convention engaged in writing a constitution not to be embroiled in daily politics and problems of government. And it is hard to live voluntarily under restraint. In complex societies, or in times of crisis, either government or people or some part of the people may feel obliged to go beyond the limits that a constitution has laid down.

In reality, the idea of the people as a constituent power, with its corollaries, developed unclearly, gradually, and sporadically during the American Revolution. It was adumbrated in the Declaration of Independence: the people may "institute new government." Jefferson, among the leaders, perhaps conceived the idea most clearly. It is of especial interest, however, to see how the "people" themselves, that is, certain lesser and unknown or poorer or unsatisfied persons, contributed to these distinctive American ideas by their opposition to the Revolutionary elite.

There were naturally many Americans who felt that no change was needed except expulsion of the British. With the disappearance of the British governors, and collapse of the old governor's councils, the kind of men who had been active in the colonial assemblies, and who now sat as provincial congresses or other *de facto* revolutionary bodies, were easily inclined to think that they should keep the management of affairs in their own hands. Some parallel can be seen with what happened in Europe. There was a revolution, or protest, of constituted bodies against authorities set above them, and a more popular form of revolution, or protest, which aimed at changing the character or membership of these constituted bodies themselves. . . . In America in 1776, the assemblies that drove out the officers of the King, and governed their respective states under revolutionary conditions, sought to keep control of affairs in their own hands, and to avoid reconstitution at the hands of the "people."

Ten states gave themselves new constitutions in 1776 and 1777. In nine of these states, however, it was the ordinary assembly, that is, the revolutionary government of the day, that drafted and proclaimed the constitution. In the tenth, Pennsylvania, a constituent convention met, but it soon had to take on the burden of daily government in addition. In Connecticut and Rhode Island the colonial charters remained in force, and the authorities constituted in colonial times (when governors and councils had already been elected) remained unchanged in principle for half a century. In Massachusetts the colonial charter remained in effect until 1780.

Thus in no state, when independence was declared, did a true constituent convention meet, and, as it were, calmly and rationally devise government out of a state of nature. There was already, however, some recognition of the principle that constitutions cannot be made merely by governments, that a more fundamental power is needed to produce a constitution than to pass ordinary laws or carry on ordinary executive duties. Thus, in New Hampshire, New York, Delaware, Maryland, North Carolina, and Georgia, the assemblies drew up constitutions only after soliciting authority for that purpose from the voters. In Maryland and North Carolina there was a measure of popular ratification. . . .

The most interesting case [of constitution making] is that of Massachusetts where the great political thinker was John Adams, who became the main author of the Massachusetts constitution of 1780, which in turn had an influence on the Constitution of the United States. In his own time Adams was denounced as an Anglomaniac and a Monocrat. In our own time some sympathizers with the eighteenth-century democrats have considered him very conservative, while on the other hand theorists of the "new conservatism" would persuade us that John Adams was in truth the American Edmund Burke. I confess that I see very little in any of these allegations.

Adams in January 1776 published some *Thoughts on Government,* for the guidance of those in the various colonies who were soon to declare independence and begin to govern themselves. This was in some ways a conservative tract. Adams thought it best, during the war, for the new states simply to keep the forms of government that they had. He obviously approved the arrangement under the Massachusetts charter of 1691, by which the popular assembly elected an upper house or council. In other ways he was not very conservative. He declared, like Jefferson, that the aim of government is welfare or happiness, that republican institutions must rest on "virtue," and that the people should support a universal system of public schools. He wanted one-year terms for governors and officials (the alternative would be "slavery"), and he favored rotation of office. He quite agreed that someday the state governors and councillors might be popularly elected, as they were in Connecticut al-

ready. He gave six reasons for having a bicameral legislature, but in none of these six reasons did he show any fear of the people, or belief that, with a unicameral legislature, the people would plunder property or degenerate into anarchy. He was afraid of the one-house legislature itself. He never committed the folly of identifying the deputies with the deputizers. He was afraid that a single house would be arbitrary or capricious, or make itself perpetual, or "make laws for their own interest, and adjudge all controversies in their own favor." He himself cited the cases of Holland and the Long Parliament. The fear of a self-perpetuating political body, gathering privileges to itself, was certainly better grounded in common observation than vague alarms about anarchy or pillage.

The *Thoughts* of 1776 were conservative in another way, if conservatism be the word. Adams had not yet conceived the idea of a constitutional convention. He lacked the notion of the people as constituent power. He had in mind that existing assemblies would draft the new constitutions, when and if any were drafted. Adams was familiar with all the high-level political theory of England and Europe. But the idea of the people as the constituent power arose locally, from the grass roots.

The revolutionary leadership in Massachusetts, including both Adamses, was quite satisfied to be rid of the British, and otherwise to keep the Bay State as it had always been. They therefore "resumed" the charter of 1691. They simply undid the Massachusetts Government Act of 1774. Some of the commonalty of Boston, and farmers of Concord and the western towns, envisaged further changes. It is hard to say what they wanted, except that they wanted a new constitution. Experts in Massachusetts history contradict each other flatly; some say that debtors, poor men, and Baptists were dissatisfied; others that all kinds of diverse people naturally owed money anyway, that practically no one was too poor to vote, and that Baptists were an infinitesimal splinter group in a solidly Congregationalist population. It may be that the trouble was basically psychological; that many people of fairly low station, even though they had long had the right to vote, had never until the Revolution participated in politics, were aroused by the Revolution, the war, and excitement of soldiering, and, feeling that affairs had always been managed by people socially above them, wanted now to act politically on their own.

Demands were heard for a new constitution. It was said that the charter of 1691 was of no force, since the royal power that had issued it was no longer valid. It was said that no one could be governed without his consent, and that no living person had really consented to this charter. Some Berkshire towns even hinted that they did not belong to Massachusetts at all until they shared in constituting the new commonwealth. They talked of "setting themselves apart," or being welcomed by a neighboring state. Echoes of the social contract floated through the western air. "The law to bind all must be assented to by all," declared the farmers of Sutton. "The Great Secret of Government is governing all by all," said those of Spencer. It began to seem that a constitution was necessary not only to secure liberty but to establish authority, not only to protect the individual but to found the state.

The house of representatives proposed that it and the council, that is, the two houses of legislation sitting together, should be authorized by the people to draw up a constitution. All adult males were to vote on the granting of this authorization, not merely those possessing the customary property qualification. In a sense, this was to

recognize Rousseau's principle that there must be "unanimity at least once": that everyone must consent to the law under which he was to live, even if later, when constitutional arrangements were made, a qualification was required for ordinary voting. . . . The plan nevertheless went through. The two houses, sitting as one, and authorized by the people, produced a constitution in 1778. It was submitted for popular ratification. The voters repudiated it. Apparently both democrats and conservatives were dissatisfied. . . .

A special election was therefore held, in which all towns chose delegates to a state convention, "for the sole purpose of forming a new Constitution." John Adams, delegate from Braintree, was put on the drafting committee. He wrote a draft, which the convention modified only in detail. The resulting document reflected many influences. It is worth while to suggest a few.

There is a modern fashion for believing that Rousseau had little influence in America, particularly on such sensible characters as John Adams. I do not think that he had very much. Adams, however, had read the *Social Contract* as early as 1765, and ultimately had four copies of it in his library. I suspect that, like others, he found much of it unintelligible or fantastic, and some of it a brilliant expression of his own beliefs. He himself said of the Massachusetts constitution: "It is Locke, Sidney, Rousseau, and de Mably reduced to practice."

Adams wrote in the preamble: "The body politic is formed by a voluntary association of individuals. It is a social compact, by which the whole people covenants with each citizen, and each citizen with the whole people, that all shall be governed by certain laws for the common good." The thought here, and the use of the word "covenant," go back to the Mayflower compact. But whence comes the "social" in *social* compact? And whence comes the word "citizen"? There were no "citizens" under the British constitution, except in the sense of freemen of the few towns known as cities. In the English language the word "citizen" in its modern sense is an Americanism, dating from the American Revolution. . . . The convention adopted this part of Adams' preamble without change.

In the enacting clause of the preamble Adams wrote: "We, therefore, the delegates of the people of Massachusetts . . . agree upon the following . . . Constitution of the Commonwealth of Massachusetts." The convention made a significant emendation: "We, therefore, the people of Massachusetts . . . agree upon, ordain and establish. . . ." The formula, *We the people ordain and establish,* expressing the developed theory of the people as constituent power, was used for the first time in the Massachusetts constitution of 1780, whence it passed into the preamble of the United States constitution of 1787 and the new Pennsylvania constitution of 1790, after which it became common in the constitutions of the new states, and in new constitutions of the old states. Adams did not invent the formula. He was content with the matter-of-fact or purely empirical statement that the "delegates" had "agreed." It was the popularly elected convention that rose to more abstract heights. Providing in advance for popular ratification, it imputed the creation of government to the people.

Adams wrote, as the first article of the Declaration of Rights: "All men are born equally free and independent, and have certain natural, essential and unalienable rights," which included defense of their lives, liberties, and property, and the seeking of "safety and happiness." The Virgin-

ia Declaration of Rights, drafted by George Mason in June 1776, was almost identical, and Adams certainly had it in mind. The Massachusetts convention made only one change in this sentence. It declared: "All men are born free and equal." The convention, obviously, was thinking of the Declaration of Independence, that is, Jefferson's more incisive rewording of Mason's Virginia declaration.

The convention had been elected by a true universal male suffrage, but it adopted, following Adams' draft, a restriction on the franchise. To vote, under the constitution, it was necessary to own real estate worth £3 a year, or real and personal property of a value of £60. The charter of 1691 had specified only £2 and £40 respectively. The state constitution was thus in this respect more conservative than the charter. How much more conservative? Here we run into the difference between experts already mentioned. A whole school of thought, pointing to a 50 per cent increase in the voting qualification, has seen a reaction of property-owners against dangers from below. Closer examination of the values of money reveals that the £3 and £60 of 1780 represent an increase of only one-eighth over the figures of 1691. Even if half the people of Boston were unfranchised, all Boston then had only a twentieth of the population of the state. In the rural areas, where farm ownership was usual, it was mainly grown sons living for a few years with their parents who lacked the vote. There seems to have been only sporadic objection to the suffrage provision.

Adams put into the constitution, and the convention retained it, that ghost of King, Lords, and Commons that now assumed the form of governor, senate, and house of representatives. Partisans of the British system, in England or America, would surely find this ghost highly attenuated. The point about King and Lords, in the British system, was precisely that they were not elected by anyone, that they were immune to popular pressure, or any pressure, through their enjoyment of life tenure and hereditary personal rights to political position. Governor and senators in Massachusetts, like representatives, both in Adams' draft and in the final document, were all elected, all by the same electorate, and all for one-year terms. To Adams ... it was of the utmost importance to prevent the executive from becoming the mere creature of the legislature. He even wished the governor to have an absolute veto, which the convention changed to a veto that could be overridden by a two-thirds majority of both houses. Adams continued to prefer a final veto. Jeffersonians and their numerous progeny found this highly undemocratic. In all states south of New York, at the end of the Revolution, governors were elected by the legislative houses, and none had any veto. Adams justified the veto as a means "to preserve the independence of the executive and judicial departments." And since governors could no longer be appointed by the crown, an obvious way to prevent their dependence on legislatures was to have them issue, like legislators, from the new sovereign, the people. It was legislative oligarchy that Adams thought the most imminent danger. As he wrote to Jefferson in 1787: "You are afraid of the one—I, of the few."

As for the phantom "lords," or senators, though they were directly elected by the ordinary voters for one-year terms, they were in a way supposed to represent property rather than numbers. They were apportioned among the counties of Massachusetts not according to population but according to taxes paid, that is, according to assessed value of taxable wealth. ... Inequalities in wealth in Massachusetts, as

between individuals or as between city and country, were not yet great enough to make a senate apportioned according to "property" (which included the small man's property as well as the rich man's) very different from a senate apportioned according to numbers.

The Massachusetts constitution prescribed certain qualifications for eligibility. The governor was required to have a freehold worth at least £1,000, senators a freehold of £300 or £600 total estate, representatives a freehold of £100 or £200 total estate. (British law at this time required £300 or £600 *annual income* from land to qualify for the House of Commons.) These Massachusetts requirements resembled those in North Carolina, where the governor had to have a £1,000 freehold, and members of the upper and lower houses freeholds of 300 or 100 acres respectively. In the absence of comparative statistics on land values and distribution of land ownership in the two states, it is impossible to compare the real impact of these legal qualifications for office. In Massachusetts, however, whatever may have been true in North Carolina, the average 100-acre one-family farm was worth well over £300, and there were a great many such farms, so that the ordinary successful farmer could qualify for either house of the legislature, and a few well-to-do ones in almost every village might if they chose have aspired to the office of governor. The requirements in Massachusetts, as set forth by John Adams, were, if anything, Jeffersonian or agrarian in their tendency, since they favored the farm population, and made it even harder for middle-class townspeople, who might own no land, to occupy public office. The aim was clearly to limit office to the substantial segment of the population, but the substantial segment was broadly defined. Still, there were people who by this definition were not "substantial," and some of them objected to these provisions, though not many would in any case have ventured to run for office or been elected if they did, in the Massachusetts of 1780.

It was Article III of the Declaration of Rights, both in Adams' draft and in the finished constitution, that caused most debate in the convention and most disagreement among the voters during ratification. This article, declaring religion to be the foundation of morality and of the state, authorized the legislature to "enjoin" people to go to church, and required the use of public funds to maintain the churches, while allowing any "subject" to have his own contribution paid to the denomination of his choice. While it received a large majority of the popular vote, 8,885 to 6,225, it was the one article which most clearly failed to obtain a two-thirds majority, and the one which may have never been legally ratified, though declared so by the convention. Those voting against it expressed a desire to separate church and state. These, in turn, included perhaps a few Baptists who favored such separation on religious principle, a great many Protestants who feared that the article might legalize Roman Catholicism, and an unknown number of people, one suspects, who were no longer very regular in attending any church at all.

The Massachusetts constitution of 1780 was adopted by a two-thirds majority in a popular referendum from which no free adult male was excluded. The vote was light, for opinion on the matter seems not to have been excited. It was six years since the rebellion against King George, and four years since the British army had left Massachusetts; doubtless many people wished to be bothered no longer. The action of the people as constituent power is, after all, a legal concept, or even a necessary legal fiction where the sovereignty of

any concrete person or government is denied. It does not signify that everyone is actually engrossed in the fabrication of constitutions. On the other hand, it does not seem necessary to believe that the convention, when it declared the constitution ratified, put something over on an innocent or apathetic or reluctant people. The people of Massachusetts had rejected the constitution proposed in 1778. They could have rejected the one proposed in 1780. It was adopted, not because it was thought perfect or final by everyone, but because it offered a frame of government, or basis of agreement, within which people could still lawfully disagree. . . .

In conclusion, the American Revolution was really a revolution, in that certain Americans subverted their legitimate government, ousted the contrary-minded and confiscated their property, and set the example of a revolutionary program, through mechanisms by which the people was deemed to act as the constituent power. This much being said, it must be admitted that the Americans, when they constituted their new states, tended to reconstitute much of what they already had. They were as fortunate and satisfied a people as any the world has known. They thus offered both the best and the worst example, the most successful and the least pertinent precedent, for less fortunate or more dissatisfied peoples who in other parts of the world might hope to realize the same principles.

Pennsylvania and Georgia gave themselves one-chamber legislatures, but both had had one-chamber legislatures before the Revolution. All states set up weak governors; they had been undermining the authority of royal governors for generations. South Carolina remained a planter oligarchy before and after independence, but even in South Carolina fifty-acre freeholders had a vote, New York set up one of the most conservative of the state constitutions, but this was the first constitution under which Jews received equality of civil rights—not a very revolutionary departure, since Jews had been prospering in New York since 1654. The Anglican Church was disestablished, but it had had few roots in the colonies anyway. In New England the sects obtained a little more recognition, but Congregationalism remained favored by law. The American revolutionaries made no change in the laws of indentured servitude. They deplored, but avoided, the matter of Negro slavery. Quitrents were generally abolished, but they had been nominal anyway, and a kind of manorial system remained long after the Revolution in New York. Laws favoring primogeniture and entail were done away with, but apparently they had been little used by landowners in any case. No general or statistical estimate is yet possible on the disposition of loyalist property. Some of the confiscated estates went to strengthen a new propertied class, some passed through the hands of speculators, and some either immediately or eventually came into the possession of small owners. There was enough change of ownership to create a material interest in the Revolution, but obviously no such upheaval in property relations as in France after 1789.

Even the apparently simple question of how many people received the right to vote because of the Revolution cannot be satisfactorily answered. There was some extension of democracy in this sense, but the more we examine colonial voting practices the smaller the change appears. The Virginia constitution of 1776 simply gave the vote to those "at present" qualified. By one estimate the number of persons voting in Virginia actually declined from 1741 to 1843, and those casting a vote in the 1780's were about a quarter of the free male population over twenty-one years of age. The

advance of political democracy, at the time of the Revolution, was most evident in the range of officers for whom voters could vote. In the South the voters generally voted only for members of the state legislatures; in Pennsylvania and New England they voted also for local officials, and in New England for governors as well.

In 1796, at the time of the revolution in Europe, and when the movement of Jeffersonian democracy was gathering strength in America, seven of the sixteen states then in the union had no property qualification for voters in the choice of the lower legislative house, and half of them provided for popular election of governors, only the seaboard South, and New Jersey, persisting in legislative designation of the executive. . . . The truth seems to be that America was a good deal more democratic than Europe in the 1790s. It had been so, within limits, long before the revolutionary era began.

Nor in broad political philosophy did the American Revolution require a violent break with customary ideas. For Englishmen it was impossible to maintain, in the eighteenth century or after, that the British constitution placed any limits on the powers of Parliament. Not so for Americans; they constantly appealed, to block the authority of Parliament or other agencies of the British government, to their rights as Englishmen under the British constitution. The idea of limited government, the habit of thinking in terms of two levels of law, of an ordinary law checked by a higher constitutional law, thus came out of the realities of colonial experience. The colonial Americans believed also, like Blackstone for that matter, that the rights of Englishmen were somehow the rights of all mankind. When the highest English authorities disagreed on what Americans claimed as English rights, and when the Americans ceased to be English by abjuring their King, they were obliged to find another and less ethnocentric or merely historical principle of justification. They now called their rights the rights of man. Apart from abstract assertions of natural liberty and equality, which were not so much new and alarming as conceptual statements as in the use to which they were applied, the rights claimed by Americans were the old rights of Englishmen—trial by jury, *habeas corpus,* freedom of the press, freedom of religion, freedom of elections, no taxation without representation. The content of rights was broadened, but the content changed less than the form, for the form now became universal. Rights were demanded for human beings as such. It was not necessary to be English, or even American, to have an ethical claim to them. The form also became more concrete, less speculative and metaphysical, more positive and merely legal. Natural rights were numbered, listed, written down, and embodied in or annexed to constitutions, in the foundations of the state itself.

So the American Revolution remains ambivalent. If it was conservative, it was also revolutionary, and vice versa. It was conservative because colonial Americans had long been radical by general standards of Western Civilization. It was, or appeared, conservative because the deepest conservatives, those most attached to King and empire, conveniently left the scene. It was conservative because the colonies had never known oppression, excepting always for slavery—because, as human institutions go, America had always been free. It was revolutionary because the colonists took the risks of rebellion, because they could not avoid a conflict among themselves, and because they checkmated those Americans who, as the country developed, most admired the aristocratic society of England and Europe. Henceforth the United States, in Louis Hartz's phrase, would be the land of the frustrated aristocrat, not of the frustrated democrat; for to be an aristocrat it is not enough to think of oneself as such, it is necessary to be thought so by others; and never again would deference for social rank be a characteristic American attitude. Elites, for better or for worse, would henceforth be on the defensive against popular values. Moreover the Americans in the 1770's, not content merely to throw off an outside authority, insisted on transmuting the theory of their political institutions. Their revolution was revolutionary because it showed how certain abstract doctrines, such as the rights of man and the sovereignty of the people, could be "reduced to practice," as Adams put it, by assemblages of fairly level-headed gentlemen exercising constituent power in the name of the people. And, quite apart from its more distant repercussions, it was certainly revolutionary in its impact on the contemporary world across the Atlantic.

Much of the recent scholarship concerning revolutionary political thought has focused on the emergence of a new and dynamic republican ideology during the years following 1775. GORDON S. WOOD (b. 1933), professor of American history at Brown University, has contributed perhaps more than anyone to our understanding of the freshness and compelling force of this republican world view. In the following essay, he explains both its ideological and its truly revolutionary character. One of the revolutionary generation's chief intellectual tasks, he notes, was to reconcile republicanism's central tenet of the public good with a potentially conflicting emphasis on the natural right of individuals to their own "life, liberty and the pursuit of happiness"—in short, to harmonize public responsibilities with private rights and desires. Under what conditions are these seemingly exclusive values likely to be in opposition? In agreement?*

Gordon S. Wood

Republicanism as a Revolutionary Ideology

In many ways the American Revolution was unlike any other revolution in modern western history. But in one important, even crucial, respect it was similar. The one identifying feature of a revolutionary movement, as students of revolutions have suggested, is the presence of an ideology, a set of ideas involving a fundamental shift in values which is used to mobilize the society into revolution. Apart from what may have happened politically or socially, in this one essential characteristic the American Revolution resembled every other major revolution in western history: it possessed a comprehensive and utopian revolutionary ideology with profound and even extravagant social implications. It is prob-

ably not too much to say that this American revolutionary ideology was just as much a system of ideas for fundamentally reshaping the character of the society as were the ideologies of those other revolutions. This ideology, this plan for changing the basic values of American society, was summed up by the conception of republicanism.

The intellectual sources of this republican ideology were diverse and complicated. As recent students of 18th century American thought are demonstrating, the Americans' ideas were drawn from their own indigenous Puritan heritage, from classical antiquity, and perhaps most important from the Commonwealth tradition

*Chicago Speech, copyright 1967 by Gordon S. Wood. Paper delivered before the Organization of American Historians, April 1967, Chicago, Illinois.

of English Whiggism—all set within a framework of 18th century Enlightenment rationalism. It is this Enlightenment framework—the 18th century's attempt to formulate a science of human behavior that would match that of the natural world—that connects and relates the various strands of thought and that ultimately explains the revolutionary significance of the Americans' venture into republicanism.

Republicanism meant more for Americans than a political system, more than merely elective governments; it necessarily involved a particular kind of social system as well. The 18th century, unlike the 19th century, never discussed politics apart from society, but integrated the two into what the 20th century is busy rediscovering as political sociology. At the heart of this 18th century political sociology was the belief that the form of government must be adapted to the manners and customs of the people. "As the interests of people vary with their circumstances," declared one early eighteenth-century pamphlet republished in American in 1775, "so the Form of Government may be various, yet each be best in its Proper Place, and by consequence one Form of Government may be best for this People, another for that . . ." There was nothing unusual about Montesquieu's notion that the various ideal types of governments were related to different social and cultural characteristics. Of all the various kinds of government a republic was acknowledged by most liberal intellectuals to be by far the most desirable, because it rested totally on the suffrages of the people and had by definition, *res publica*, no other end than the welfare of the people. Yet precisely because it was so utterly dependent on the people it was also the state most sensitive to changes in the character of its society and hence the most

fragile kind of polity. In a word, a republic was the state most liable to premature political death.

To the 18th century mind the decay and death of states seemed as scientifically grounded as the decay and death of human beings. Indeed, for all of its talk of contracts, the 18th century generally still conceived of the state in organic terms: "It is with states as it is with men," was a commonplace of the day; "they have their infancy, their manhood, and their decline." The history of particular nations and peoples, whatever may have been the history of civilization as a whole, was not a linear progression, but a variable cycle of birth, maturity and death, in which bodies politic, like the human body, carried within themselves the seeds of their own dissolution, "which ripen faster or slower," depending on the changing character of the society. The study of this life cycle in states, particularly focusing on political disease, was of central concern to the Enlightenment, for through such "political pathology," as one American aptly called it, men could hopefully further their knowledge of political medicine and retard the process of decay.

With these kinds of concerns the whole world, including the past, became a kind of laboratory in which the sifting and evaluating of empirical evidence would lead to an understanding of social sickness and health. Political science thus became a kind of diagnostics, which helps to explain the Americans' remarkable attempt to determine the state of Britain's health in the mid-18th century. In a like way history became a kind of autopsy of the past, an autopsy of those bodies politic which had died, of which the most important were obviously the great republics of antiquity. The decline and fall of the ancient republics was a fascinating subject to the 18th century, the kind that commencement speakers at American colleges in the 1770's could scarcely resist. For "the moss-grown columns and broken arches of those once renowned empires," as one American put it, "are full with instruction" for a people attempting to rebuild a republican world. Out of their reading of the Latin classics, particularly those of what Peter Gay has called the Roman Enlightenment, and out of contemporary histories of the ancient world, like Charles Rollin's popular studies, mingled with ideas drawn from the English classical republican tradition and 17th century Puritanism, all firmly grounded in Enlightenment science, the Americans put together a conception of the ideal society they would have to have if they would sustain their republican revolution.

It was not the force of arms which had made the ancient republics great, nor was it military might which had destroyed them. It was rather the spirit of their people which was ultimately responsible both for the prosperity and the eventual misery of the classical republics. The Roman Republic had attained the heights it did because its people, "instructed from early infancy to deem themselves the property of the State," had continually been willing to surrender their private interests and pleasures to the greater good of the whole society. This spartan spirit of self-sacrifice for the common welfare—this compelling love of country or patriotism—the 18th century called public virtue, the most vital quality a people could possess. Every state like England in which the people participated required some public virtue, but a republic which rested solely on the people absolutely required it. Although a particular structural arrangement of the government in a republic, like a bicameral legislature and a strong governor, might temper the

necessity for public virtue, ultimately "no model of government whatever can equal the importance of this principle, nor afford proper safety and security without it."

In a monarchy the complicated texture of the society and the vigor of the unitary authority, often with the aid of a standing army and an established religious hierarchy, reduced the need for virtue; fear and force alone could be used to restrain each man's desire to do what was right in his own eyes. In a republic, however, which possessed no intricate social pattern and where the elected rulers were "in fact the servants of the public" and known by all "to be but men," there was no place for fear or sustained coercion from above. Each man must somehow be persuaded to submerge his selfish wants into the greater good of the whole. In a republic, said John Adams, "all things must give way to the public." "A Citizen," declared Samuel Adams, "owes everything to the Commonwealth." "Every man in a republic," wrote Benjamin Rush, "is public property. His time and talents—his youth—his manhood—his old age—nay more, life, all belong to his country." In a republic then "each individual gives up all private interest that is not consistent with the general good, the interest of the whole body," the public good, as it was generally called.

No phrase except liberty was invoked more often by the Revolutionaries than this term the public good. It, as much as liberty, defined the goals of the Revolution. It was a central tenet of the Whig faith, shared not only by Hamilton and Paine at opposite ends of the Whig spectrum, but by any American bitterly opposed to a system which held "that a Part is greater than its whole; or, in other Words, that some Individuals ought to be considered, even to the Destruction of the Community, which they compose." This emphasis on the collective welfare as the goal of politics helps to explain the Revolutionary generation's aversion to faction. And it also makes sense of the Revolutionaries' belief in the impossibility of maintaining a republic over a large area and a heterogeneous population. For politics in a republican state was conceived to be not the reconciling but the transcending of the different interests of the community; it was the discovery and promotion of the unitary common interest, like Rousseau's general will, which only a relatively small homogeneous community could sustain.

Republicanism thus emphasized a morality of social cohesion and promised the kind of organic state where men were indissolubly linked one to another in harmony and benevolence. "The public good is, as it were, a common bank in which every individual has his respective share; and consequently whatever damage that sustains, the individual unavoidably partakes of that calamity." Public virtue or unselfish devotion to this collective good represented all that men of the 18th century, from Edwards to Franklin, sought in social behavior. The "grand source" of this public virtue, "this endearing and benevolent passion," lay in the attitudes and actions of the individuals who made up the society. In other words, those who would be most willing to forego their selfish interests for the public good were those who individually practiced what were a mixture of classical and Protestant virtues—temperance, industry, frugality, simplicity, and charity—the virtues of the classical patriot, the Puritan saint, and the sturdy rustic yeoman, all intermingled. While some men of the 18th century could see public virtue arising out of the individual's pride and need for approbation, few endorsed Mandeville's paradoxical view that private vices produced public virtue. For

most Americans in 1776 vicious behavior by an individual could have only disastrous results for the community. A man racked by the selfish passions of greed, envy, and hate lost his conception of order; "his sense of connection with the *general* system—his benevolence—his desire and freedom of *doing good* ceased." Only men who were industrious and content in their mediocrity, only men who had no desire to set themselves off from their fellow citizens by refinements and wealth, would be willing to sacrifice their individual desires for the common good.

While the Romans for example, as American orators and writers repeatedly explained, maintained their simplicity of manners, their scorn of artificial distinctions, and their recognition of true merit, they raised their state to the heights of glory. But they stretched their conquests too far, and their Asiatic wars brought them wealth they had never known before. "From that moment virtue and public spirit sunk apace: dissipation vanished temperance and independence." Men became obsessed with luxury, with "Grandeur and Magnificence in Buildings, of Sumptuousness and Delicacy in their Tables, of Richness and Pomp in their Dress, of Variety and Singularity in their Furniture." Such love of luxury widened the gap between rich and poor and tore the society with faction and violence. It was no longer merit that raised men up to the first employments of the state, but "the chance of birth, and the caprice of fortune." From an austere and hardy people, "accustomed to the Forts of War, and Agriculture," the Romans, as Sallust and Plutarch only too grimly described, became a soft and effeminate people, concerned only with "a pretended fine taste for all the Refinements of a voluptuous Life." When a republic reached this point, when its people were no longer willing or able to serve the state, then dissolution had to follow.

The lesson then for the Americans was obvious: not only did the fall of the ancient states explain the fate of Britain in the mid-18th century but it warned the Americans of the extraordinary kind of people they would have to be if they would establish and maintain their new republic governments. Their revolution thus necessarily involved a radical social adjustment as well as a political transformation—an alteration in their very behavior, "laying the foundation in a constitution not without or over, but within the subject." When the Americans of 1776 talked about their intention to "form a new era and give a new turn to human affairs" by becoming the "eminent examples of every divine and social virtue," they meant that they would become the special kind of unselfish, egalitarian, and virtuous people that history and social science said was needed to sustain a republic. The moral quality of their social character thus became the measure of the success of their Revolution.

However chimerical such hopes for American virtue may seem in retrospect, the Revolutionaries in 1776 had reason for confidence, in fact had reason to believe that they were "aptly circumstanced to form the best republicks, upon the best terms that ever came to the lot of any people before us." Throughout the 18th century the Americans had been repeatedly told by European intellectuals that they were a peculiarly virtuous people, especially fit for republicanism. In the minds of French Philosophes and English radicals alike the New World had become "a mirage in the West," a symbol of their dream of new order and a weapon in their fight against the decadence of the ancient regimes. America seemed to consist, wrote Richard Price, "of only a body of yeomanry supported by agriculture, and all independent, and nearly upon a level." England, in contrast, was old and withered; "inflated and irreligious; enervated by luxury; encumbered by debts, and hanging by a thread." When in the controversy with England Americans were forced to search their souls to find out the kind of people they were, they could not help but be dazzled by the portrait, so "very flattering to us," that these "many worthy patrons beyond the Atlantic" had painted of them. Everywhere they looked there was confirmation of what the philosophes and English radicals had said about them.

All through the 60's and 70's Americans told themselves over and over that they were a sober, egalitarian, industrious people, who were "strangers to that luxury which effeminates the mind and body." "The Americans," said William Henry Drayton, "now live without luxury. They are habituated to despise their yearly profits by agriculture and trade. They engage in war from principle. . . . From such a people everything is to be hoped for, nothing is to be doubted of." Everywhere the colonists were suffering personal injuries and depravations for the cause of their country, moreso, said the Rev. Isaac Mansfield, "than in any given term of time before; no threatening quarrels, or animosities have subsisted; but harmony and internal peace have ever reigned, and one soul has inspired the body politic." And all this at a time, John Page told Jefferson, "when they were free from the Restraint of Laws." By obeying the nonimportation agreements and the resolves of the Continental and provincial congresses, although they lacked the force of law, the Americans were amply demonstrating, said Peter Thacher, "that a spirit of public virtue may transcend every private consideration." James Iredell, no fanatic, was astonished at the peace and order of the people during the long suspension of the courts, "an instance of regularity," he believed, "not to be equalled, in similar circumstances, by any other people under heaven." This, he could only hope, was "a happy presage of that virtue which is to support our present government." This period of great self-denial and order without formal governments, those years just prior to the Declaration of Independence, marked the time and spirit which best defined the aims of the Revolutionaries and to which they looked back with increasing nostalgia.

For all of this confidence in the peculiarity of their virtue, however, Americans were well aware that their colonial society had not been all that the Enlightenment believed it to be, that they had not really been free of the vices and luxury of the Old World. Indeed, even to those who dwelled on America's distinctiveness, it appeared quite the contrary. America, declared some on the eve of the Revolution, "never was, perhaps, in a more corrupt and degenerate State than at this Day." In the eyes of many Americans, whether Southern planters or New England clergy, the society was far from virtuous and in fact seemed to be approaching some sort of crisis in its development. But the prevalence of vice and corruption that many Americans saw in their midst did not work to restrain their desire to be republican. It became in fact a stimulus, perhaps in the end the most important stimulus, to revolution. What ultimately convinced Americans that they must revolt in 1776 was not that they were naturally and inevitably republican, for if that were truly the case evolution and not revolution would have been the eventual solution. Rather it was the pervasive fear that they might not be

pre-destined to be a virtuous and egalitarian people after all that finally drove them into revolution in 1776. It was this fear, and not their confidence in the peculiarity of their character, that made them so readily and so remarkably responsive to Thomas Paine's warning that the time for independence was at hand and that delay would be disastrous. By 1776 it had become increasingly evident that if they were to be a virtuous people they must become free of Britain.

What we would call the signs of the maturation of colonial society in the middle 18th century seemed to many Americans to be symptoms of regression. "To increase in numbers, in wealth, in elegance and refinements, and at the same time to increase in luxury, profaneness, impiety, and a disesteem of things sacred, is to go backward and not forward." Never before had corruption and the scramble for luxury seemed so prevalent, especially since the war with France. Everywhere men appeared to be seeking the preferment of royal authority, eager to sell their country "for a smile, or some ministerial office." The effects of an expanding capitalistic economy and the apparent emergence of an artificial intercolonial aristocracy springing ultimately from the honors and benefits bestowed by the Crown—were described in frightened tones. Throughout all the colonies and rising to a fever pitch by 1775–76 were strident warnings in newspapers, pamphlets, and sermons of the great social changes threatening American virtue and equality that were sweeping the land.

While some Americans found the source of these social changes in their own wantonness as a people, others increasingly came to attribute what was happening to their society to their connection to the corrupted English monarchy. "Alas! Great Britain," declared one Virginian in 1775, "their vices have even extended to America! . . . The Torrent as yet is but small; only a few are involved in it; it must be stopped, or it will bear all before it with an impetuous sway." By the 60's and 70's the multiplication of wealth and luxury, the attempts to harden the social hierarchy, particularly the efforts of those who considered themselves socially superior to set themselves off from the rest of American society by aping the "Asiatic amusements" of English court life—all seemed to be part of the Crown's conspiracy to numb and enervate the spirit of the American people. England, it seemed, was encouraging American "dissipation and extravagance" both to increase the sale of her manufactures and geegaws and to perpetuate American subordination. "In vain," recalled David Ramsay in 1778, "we sought to check the growth of luxury, by sumptuary laws; every wholesome restraint of this kind was sure to meet with the royal negative." If Americans had not eventually revolted, concluded Ramsay, "our frugality, industry, and simplicity of manners, would have been lost in an imitation of British extravagance, idleness, and false refinements."

Since these social developments threatened the Americans' very capacity to be a free people, the controversy with England assumed a particular timeliness and the call for independence took on a tone of imperativeness. In August 1776 Charles Thompson told John Dickinson that he was fully persuaded, from the prevailing "prejudices" and from "the notions of honor, rank & other courtly ideas so eagerly embraced," that "had time been given for them to strike deeper root, it would have been extremely difficult to have prepared men's minds for the good seed of liberty." "Let our harbours, our doors, our hearts, be shut against luxury" became the common exhortation of Calvinist preachers and Enlightenment rationalists alike. The clergy could not help noting with obvious satisfaction that their traditional Puritan jeremiads were now being reinforced by the best social science of the 18th century. So as "pride, prodigality, and extravagance" were vices "contrary to the spirit of religion, and highly provoking to Heaven, so they also, in the natural course of things, tend to bring poverty and ruin upon a people." Hence, "the light of nature and revelation," Enlightenment rationalism and Christian theology—perhaps for a final moment at the end of the 18th century—were firmly united in their understanding of what was needed for the reformation of American society. Religion and republicanism would work hand in hand to create frugality, honesty, self-denial and benevolence among the people. The city upon the hill assumed a new republican character. It would now hopefully be, in Samuel Adams' revealing words, "the Christian Sparta."

Republicanism, however, was to be more than just a response to this promised reformation of American society; it was itself to be an agent of regeneration. There was, the 18th century believed, a reciprocating relationship between the form of government and the spirit of its society. It was this belief in the mutual influence, the feedback and interplay, between the character of the government and the character of the people that makes many 18th century intellectuals like Montesquieu so subtle and elusive. On one hand, there was no doubt that the nature of the government must be adapted to the customs and habits of the people. Yet on the other hand politics was not simply a matter of social determinism; the form of government was not simply a passive expression of what the spirit of the people dictated. "It is the Form of Government," said John Adams, "which gives the decisive colour to the

Manners of the People, more than any other thing." Hence if the Americans wanted to be a hardy virtuous and egalitarian people, a republican government would be the best means for becoming so.

Not only would republican governments promise a new emphasis on education, a new didactic iconography, and the right kinds of laws against entail, primogeniture, and monopoly, and perhaps even excessive wealth itself, but they would inevitably alter the structure of American society. Under the electoral system of republicanism American society would be governed, as it had not been in the past, by the principle of equality—the very "life and soul" of republicanism David Ramsay called it. Equality to most Americans in 1776 was not a social levelling, although it did presume an absence of legal privilege and of great distinctions of wealth and rank. Rather it was more "an equality which is adverse to every species of subordination beside that which arises from the difference of *capacity, disposition* and *virtue.*" With the Revolution most Americans intended only to change the origin of social and political preeminence, not to do away with such preeminence altogether. "In monarchies," said Ramsay, "favor is the source of preferment; but in our new forms of government, no one can command the suffrages of the people, unless by his superior merit and capacities." Republicanism would mean careers open to talent and distinctions naturally and not artificially based. The republican society, said Charles Lee, would still possess "honour, property, and military glories," but they now would "be obtain'd without court favor, or the rascally talents of servility." Only in such an egalitarian society where, in John Adams' words, "Capacity, Spirit and Zeal in the cause, supply the Place of Fortune, Family, and every other Consideration, which used to have Weight with Mankind," only

in such a society would the people willingly follow their leaders and voluntarily surrender their private desires for the good of the whole. Equality thus represented the social source from which the anticipated harmony and public virtue of America would flow. "It is this principle of equality . . . ," as one Virginian said in 1776, "which alone can inspire and preserve the virtue of its members, by placing them in a relation to the publick and to their fellow-citizens, which has a tendency to engage the heart and the affections to both."

It was therefore not just a break from the British empire that the Americans intended in 1776, but a revolution promising extensive changes in the character and structure of their society, changes that republicanism both required and sustained at the same time. These promised changes were not simply the eccentric illusions of overly zealous clergymen or starry-eyed demagogues, but were the scientifically-based expectations of anyone in the 18th century who would establish a republican system. Different men of course expected different degrees of change and their variations in expectations were in fact a measure of their eagerness to revolt, distinguishing a confident Richard Henry Lee from a skeptical Robert Morris. There were apprehensions in 1776, many of them. Running through the correspondence of the Whig leaders are fearful suggestions of what republicanism might mean, of levelling, of licentiousness, of "the race of popularity." A sense of anxiety was never lost, even among the most optimistic like Jefferson. It was a grandiose and dangerous experiment, for they all knew how delicate a polity a republic was. Indeed, it is only in the context of this sense of uncertainty and risk that the Revolutionaries' obsessive concern with their social and moral character can be properly appreciated. They knew only too well where the real source of danger lay. "We shall succeed if we are virtuous," Samuel Adams told John Langdon in 1777. "I am infinitely more apprehensive of the Contagion of Vice than the Power of all other Enemies." Benjamin Rush in 1777 even hoped that the war would not end too soon: "A peace at this time would be the greatest curse that could befall us. . . . Liberty without virtue would be no blessing to us." Several more military campaigns were needed, he said, in order "to purge away the monarchical impurity we contracted by laying so long upon the lap of Great Britain."

Yet for all of this anxiety what in the last analysis remains extraordinary about 1776 is the faith not the doubts of the Revolutionary leaders, the faith they had in their ability to create a truly virtuous society in which the individual was important only in so far as he served the state. It was this hope of regenerating the American character and eliminating individualism and selfishness that made the Revolution such a utopian movement and gave to it its revolutionary ideology. The revolution the Americans eventually achieved was not precisely the revolution they intended and it may in fact have been more revolutionary than the original aim. But the aim itself, the ideology of republicanism, promised in 1776 such a radical transformation of American society as to make the American Revolution one of the truly great revolutions in Western history.

Revolutionary movements have a way of breaking away
from their original definitions, of expanding in new and
unforeseen ways beyond the goals initially formulated. The
essay by BERNARD BAILYN (b. 1922) emphasizes the
ways in which the dynamics of the revolutionary
experience served to radicalize American political belief.
During the revolutionary years, he is saying, there
occurred a progressive but major reorientation of the whole
political culture, with the result that existing institutions
and beliefs took on new and profound meanings. The point
is an important one, for the "radicalness" of an era may
consist as much in the redefinition of familiar ways of life
as in the creation of entirely new ones. The reader will
want to follow closely Bailyn's description of this process.
Bailyn is Winthrop Professor of American History at
Harvard.*

Bernard Bailyn

The Transforming Radicalism
of the Revolution

The primary goal of the American Revolution, which transformed American life and introduced a new era in human history, was not the overthrow or even the alteration of the existing social order but the preservation of political liberty threatened by the apparent corruption of the [English] constitution, and the establishment in principle of the existing conditions of liberty. The communication of understanding, therefore, lay at the heart of the Revolutionary movement. . . .

What was essentially involved in the American Revolution was not the disruption of society, with all the fear, despair, and hatred that that entails, but the realization, the comprehension and fulfillment, of the inheritance of liberty and of what

was taken to be America's destiny in the context of world history. The great social shocks that in the French and Russian Revolutions sent the foundations of thousands of individual lives crashing into ruins had taken place in America in the course of the previous century, slowly, silently, almost imperceptibly, not as a sudden avalanche but as myriads of individual changes and adjustments which had gradually transformed the order of society. By 1763 the great landmarks of European life—the church and the idea of orthodoxy, the state and the idea of authority: much of the array of institutions and ideas that buttressed the society of the *ancien régime*—had faded in their exposure to the open, wilderness environment of America. But until the dis-

*Reprinted by permission of the publishers from Bernard Bailyn, *The Ideological Origins of the American Revolution*. Cambridge, Mass.: The Belknap Press of Harvard University Press. Copyright 1967, by the President and Fellows of Harvard College. Pp. 19–21, 160–175, 302–310, 318–319. Footnotes omitted.

turbances of the 1760's these changes had not been seized upon as grounds for a reconsideration of society and politics. Often they had been condemned as deviations, as retrogressions back toward a more primitive condition of life. Then, after 1760—and especially in the decade after 1765—they were brought into open discussion as the colonists sought to apply advanced principles of society and politics to their own immediate problems.

The original issue of the Anglo-American conflict was, of course, the question of the extent of Parliament's jurisdiction in the colonies. But that could not be discussed in isolation. The debate involved eventually a wide range of social and political problems, and it ended by 1776 in what may be called the conceptualization of American life. By then Americans had come to think of themselves as in a special category, uniquely placed by history to capitalize on, to complete and fulfill, the promise of man's existence. The changes that had overtaken their provincial societies, they saw, had been good: elements not of deviance and retrogression but of betterment and progress; not a lapse into primitivism, but an elevation to a higher plane of political and social life than had ever been reached before. Their rustic blemishes had become the marks of a chosen people. "The liberties of mankind and the glory of human nature is in their keeping," John Adams wrote in the year of the Stamp Act. "America was designed by Providence for the theatre on which man was to make his true figure, on which science, virtue, liberty, happiness, and glory were to exist in peace."

The effort to comprehend, to communicate, and to fulfill this destiny was continuous through the entire Revolutionary generation—it did not cease, in fact, until in the nineteenth century its creative achievements became dogma. But there were

three phases of particular concentration: the period up to and including 1776, centering on the discussion of Anglo-American differences; the devising of the first state governments, mainly in the years from 1776 to 1780; and the reconsideration of the state constitutions and the reconstruction of the national government in the last half of the eighties and in the early nineties. In each of these phases important contributions were made not only to the skeletal structure of constitutional theory but to the surrounding areas of social thought as well. But in none was the creativity as great, the results as radical and as fundamental, as in the period before Independence. It was then that the premises were defined and the assumptions set. It was then that explorations were made in new territories of thought, the first comprehensive maps sketched, and routes marked out. Thereafter the psychological as well as intellectual barriers were down. It was the most creative period in the history of American political thought. Everything that followed assumed and built upon its results. . . .

It was an elevating, transforming vision: a new, fresh, vigorous, and above all morally regenerate people rising from obscurity to defend the battlements of liberty and then in triumph standing forth, heartening and sustaining the cause of freedom everywhere. In the light of such a conception everything about the colonies and their controversy with the mother country took on a new appearance. Provincialism was gone: Americans stood side by side with the heroes of historic battles for freedom and with the few remaining champions of liberty in the present. What were once felt to be defects—isolation, institutional simplicity, primitiveness of manners, multiplicity of religions, weakness in the authority of the state—could now be seen as virtues, not only by Americans themselves but by enlightened spokes-men of reform, renewal, and hope wherever they might be—in London coffee-houses, in Parisian *salons,* in the courts of German princes. The mere existence of the colonists suddenly became philosophy teaching by example. Their manners, their morals, their way of life, their physical, so-cial, and political condition were seen to vindicate eternal truths and to demon-strate, as ideas and words never could, the virtues of the heavenly city of the eighteenth-century philosophers.

But the colonists' ideas and words counted too, and not merely because they repeated as ideology the familiar utopian phrases of the Enlightenment and of En-glish libertarianism. What they were saying by 1776 was familiar in a general way to reformers and illuminati everywhere in the Western world; yet it was different. Words and concepts had been reshaped in the colo-nists' minds in the course of a decade of pounding controversy—strangely re-shaped, turned in unfamiliar directions, toward conclusions they could not them-selves clearly perceive. They found a new world of political thought as they struggled to work out the implications of their beliefs in the years before Independence. It was a world not easily possessed; often they withdrew in some confusion to more fa-miliar ground. But they touched its bound-aries, and, at certain points, probed its interior. Others, later—writing and revis-ing the first state constitutions, drafting and ratifying the federal constitution, and debating in detail, exhaustively, the merits of these efforts—would resume the search for resolutions of the problems the colonists had broached before 1776.

This critical probing of traditional con-cepts—part of the colonists' effort to ex-press reality as they knew it and to shape it to ideal ends—became the basis for all

further discussions of enlightened reform, in Europe as well as in America. The radi-calism the Americans conveyed to the world in 1776 was a transformed as well as a transforming force.

The question of representation was the first serious intellectual problem to come between England and the colonies, and while it was not the most important issue involved in the Anglo-American controver-sy (the whole matter of taxation and repre-sentation was "a mere incident," Profes-sor McIlwain has observed, in a much more basic constitutional struggle), it re-ceived the earliest and most exhaustive ex-amination and underwent a most reveal-ing transformation. This shift in concep-tion took place rapidly; it began and for all practical purposes concluded in the two years of the Stamp Act controversy. But the intellectual position worked out by the Americans in that brief span of time had deep historical roots; it crystallized, in ef-fect, three generations of political ex-perience. The ideas the colonists put for-ward, rather than creating a new condition of fact, expressed one that had long ex-isted; they articulated and in so doing gen-eralized, systematized, gave moral sanction to what had emerged haphazardly, incom-pletely and insensibly, from the chaotic factionalism of colonial politics.

What had taken place in the earlier years of colonial history was the partial re-creation, as a matter of fact and not of theory, of a kind of representation that had flourished in medieval England but that had faded and been superseded by another during the fifteenth and sixteenth cen-turies. In its original, medieval, form elec-tive representation to Parliament had been a device by which "local men, locally minded, whose business began and ended with the interests of the constituency," were enabled, as attorneys for their electors, to seek redress from the royal court of Parliament, in return for which they were expected to commit their constituents to grants of financial aid. Attendance at Parliament of representatives of the commons was for the most part an obligation unwillingly performed, and local communities bound their representatives to local interests in every way possible: by requiring local residency or the ownership of local property as a qualification for election, by closely controlling the payment of wages for official services performed, by instructing representatives minutely as to their powers and the limits of permissible concessions, and by making them strictly accountable for all actions taken in the name of the constituents. As a result, representatives of the commons in the medieval Parliaments did not speak for that estate in general or for any other body of group larger than the specific one that had elected them.

Changing circumstances, however, had drastically altered this form and practice of representation. By the time the institutions of government were taking firm shape in the American colonies, Parliament in England had been transformed. The restrictions that had been placed upon representatives of the commons to make them attorneys of their constituencies fell away; members came to sit "not merely as parochial representatives, but as delegates of all the commons of the land." Symbolically incorporating the state, Parliament in effect had become the nation for purposes of government, and its members virtually if not actually, symbolically if not by sealed orders, spoke for all as well as for the group that had chosen them. They stood for the interest of the realm; for Parliament, in the words by which Edmund Burke immortalized this whole concept of representation, was not "a *congress* of ambassadors from different and hostile interests, which

interests each must maintain, as an agent and advocate, against other agents and advocates; but Parliament is a *deliberative* assembly of *one* nation, with *one* interest, that of the whole, where, not local purposes, not local prejudices ought to guide, but the general good, resulting from the general reason of the whole." "Instructions, therefore," Speaker Onslow said, "from particular constituents to their own Members are or can be only of information, advice, and recommendation ... but not absolutely binding upon votes and actings and conscience in Parliament." The restrictions once placed upon representatives to make them attorneys of their constituencies fell away.

But the colonists, reproducing English institutions in miniature, had been led by force of circumstance to move in the opposite direction. Starting with seventeenth-century assumptions, out of necessity they drifted backward, as it were, toward medieval forms of attorneyship in representation. Their surroundings had recreated to a significant extent the conditions that had shaped the earlier experiences of the English people. The colonial towns and counties, like their medieval counterparts, were largely autonomous, and they stood to lose more than they were likely to gain from a loose acquiescence in the action of central government. More often than not they felt themselves to be the benefactors rather than the beneficiaries of central government, provincial or imperial; and when they sought favors from higher authorities they sought local and particular—in effect private—favors. Having little reason to identify their interests with those of the central government, they sought to keep the voices of local interests clear and distinct; and where it seemed necessary, they moved—though with little sense of innovating or taking actions of broad significance, and nowhere comprehensively or systematically—to bind representatives to local interests. The Massachusetts town meetings began the practice of voting instructions to their deputies to the General Court in the first years of settlement, and they continued to do so whenever it seemed useful throughout the subsequent century and a half. Elsewhere, with variations, it was the same; and elsewhere, as in Massachusetts, it became customary to require representatives to be residents of, as well as property owners in, the localities that elected them, and to check upon their actions as delegates. With the result that disgruntled contemporaries felt justified in condemning Assemblies composed "of plain, illiterate husbandmen, whose views seldom extended farther than to the regulation of highways, the destruction of wolves, wildcats, and foxes, and the advancement of the other little interests of the particular counties which they were chosen to represent."

All of this, together with the associated experience common to all of the colonies of selecting and controlling agents to speak for them in England, formed the background for the discussion of the first great issue of the Anglo-American controversy. For the principal English argument put forward in defense of Parliament's right to pass laws taxing the colonies was that the colonists, like the "nine tenths of the people of Britain" who do not choose representatives to Parliament, were in fact represented there. The power of actually voting for representatives, it was claimed, was an accidental and not a necessary attribute of representation, "for the right of election is annexed to certain species of property, to peculiar franchises, and to inhabitancy in certain places." In what really counted there was no difference between those who happened to live in England and those in America: "none are actually, all are virtually represented in Parliament," for, the argument concluded,

every Member of Parliament sits in the House not as representative of his own constituents but as one of that august assembly by which all the commons of *Great Britain* are represented. Their rights and their interests, however his own borough may be affected by general dispositions, ought to be the great objects of his attention and the only rules for his conduct, and to sacrifice these to a partial advantage in favor of the place where he was chosen would be a departure from his duty.

In England the practice of "virtual" representation provided reasonably well for the actual representation of the major interests of the society, and it raised no widespread objection. It was its opposite, the idea of representation as attorneyship, that was seen as "a new sort of political doctrine strenuously enforced by modern malcontents." But in the colonies the situation was reversed. There, where political experience had led to a different expectation of the process of representation and where the workings of virtual representation in the case at hand were seen to be damaging, the English argument was met at once with flat and universal rejection, ultimately with derision. It consists, Daniel Dulany wrote in a comprehensive refutation of the idea, "of facts not true and of conclusions inadmissible." What counts, he said in terms with which almost every writer in America agreed, was the extent to which representation worked to protect the interests of the people against the encroachments of government. From this point of view the analogy between the nonelectors in England and those in America was utterly specious, for the interests of Englishmen who did not vote for members of Parliament were intimately bound up with those who did and with those chosen to sit as representatives. The interests of all three, "the nonelectors, the electors, and the representatives, are individually the same, to say nothing of the connection among the neighbors, friends, and relations. The security of the nonelectors against oppression is that their oppression will fall also upon the electors and the representatives. The one can't be injured and the other indemnified." But no such "intimate and inseparable relation" existed between the electors of Great Britain and the inhabitants of the colonies. The two groups were by no means involved in the same consequences of taxation: "not a single actual elector in England might be immediately affected by a taxation in America imposed by a statute which would have a general operation and effect upon the properties of the inhabitants of the colonies."

Once a lack of natural identity of interests between representatives and the populace was conceded, the idea of virtual representation lost any force it might have had; for by such a notion, James Otis wrote, you could "as well prove that the British House of Commons in fact represent all the people of the globe as those in America." The idea, in such situations, was "futile" and "absurd"—the work of a "political visionary." It was a notion, Arthur Lee wrote, with supporting quotations from Bolingbroke, Locke, Sidney, Camden, Pulteney, Petyt, Sir Joseph Jekyll, and assorted Parliamentary speakers, that "would, in the days of superstition, have been called witchcraft," for what it means is that while "our privileges are all *virtual,* our sufferings are *real . . .* We might have flattered ourselves that a *virtual obedience* would have exactly corresponded with a *virtual representation,* but it is the ineffable wisdom of Mr. Grenville to reconcile what, to our feeble comprehensions, appeared to

be contradictions, and therefore a *real* obedience is required to this *virtual* power." Who, precisely, is the American freeman's virtual representative in England?

Does he know us? Or we him? No. Have we any restriction over his conduct? No. Is he bound in duty and interest to preserve our liberty and property? No. Is he acquainted with our circumstances, situation, wants, &c.? No. What then are we to expect from him? Nothing but taxes without end.

. . . But the colonists' discussion of representation did not stop with the refutation of the claims made for virtual representation. The debate broadened into a general consideration of the nature and function of representation—in situations where interests of electors and elected, franchised and disfranchised, coincided as well as where they did not. The virtues of binding representatives by instructions were now explicitly explored. Some approached the question cautiously, arguing that, though the idea "that the constituent can bind his representative by instructions" may in recent years have become "an unfashionable doctrine," nevertheless, "in most cases" the "persuasive influence" if not the "obligatory force" of instructions should be insisted upon: "a representative who should act against the explicit recommendation of his constituents would most deservedly forfeit their regard and all pretension to their future confidence." But the dominant voices were direct and decisive. The right to instruct representatives, Arthur Lee declared in the fourth of his "Monitor" papers, has been denied only "since the system of corruption which is now arrived to so dangerous a heighth began first to predominate in our constitution. Then it was that arbitrary ministers and their prostituted dependents began to maintain this doctrine dangerous to our liberty, that the representatives were independent of the people. This was necessary to serve their own tyrannical and selfish purposes." Elected representatives, he stated, "are *trustees for their constituents* to transact for them the business of government ... and for this *service* they, like all other agents, were paid by their constituents, till they found it more advantageous to sell their voices in Parliament, and then ... wished to become independent of the people." Defended, he wrote, by all the great authorities from Demosthenes to Coke, its denial condemned by Sir William Wyndham as "the most monstrous, the most slavish doctrine that was ever heard," the right of freemen not merely to choose representatives but to bind them with instructions "must have begun with the constitution," and was "an ancient and unalienable right in the people." The fact that "Mr. Blackstone, in his commentary on the law of England, has asserted the contrary" carried no weight with him. It was enough to point out that Blackstone "founds his opinion on that fiction of a person's being, after he is elected, the representative of the whole kingdom, and not of a particular part. The sophistry of this argument is sufficiently manifest, and has been fully exploded. The British constitution is not to be new modelled by every *court* lawyer. [*footnote*:] *Mr. Blackstone is solicitor to the Queen.*" Constituents, it was agreed, had nothing less than "an inherent right to give instructions to their representatives." For representatives, James Wilson concluded, were properly to be considered the "creatures" of their constituents, and they were to be held strictly "accountable for the use of that power which is delegated unto them."

But what did that mean? There were far-reaching implications, some of which, first drawn out during this decade of debate, would remain persistent problems until finally resolved in the realization of

American democracy in the nineteenth and twentieth centuries. It was seen, even in the 1760's and 1770's, that if a representative were kept to strict accountability, he would in effect be acting "in every respect as the persons who appointed him ... would do were they present themselves." With the result, it was concluded, that a representative assembly "should be in miniature an exact portrait of the people at large. It should think, feel, reason, and act like them." If the population shifted in composition, so too should the character of the assembly, for "equal interest among the people should have equal interest in it." There might well be, in fact, "some permanent ratio by which the representatives should ... increase or decrease with the number of inhabitants."

And what if such were the case? The result would be, if not a wholly original contribution to advanced thought, at least a reversion to a radical concept that had long since disappeared from the mainstream of English political theory. For such arguments led to a recovery and elaboration of conceptions of government by the active and continuous consent of the governed that had flourished briefly a century earlier, during the Commonwealth period, and had then faded during the Restoration, persisting subsequently only as arguments of the most extreme radicals and of the most vociferous and intransigent leaders of the Parliamentary opposition. The view of representation developing in America implied if it did not state that direct consent of the people in government was not restricted, as Locke would have had it, to those climactic moments when government was overthrown by the people in a last final effort to defend their rights, nor even to those repeated, benign moments when a government was peaceably dissolved and another chosen in its place. Where government was such an accurate mirror of the people, sensitively reflecting their desires and feelings, consent was a continuous, everyday process. In effect the people were present through their representatives, and were themselves, step by step and point by point, acting in the conduct of public affairs. No longer merely an ultimate check on government, they *were* in some sense the government. Government had no separate existence apart from them; it was *by* the people as well as *for* the people; it gained its authority from their continuous consent. The very nature and meaning of law was involved. The traditional sense, proclaimed by Blackstone no less than by Hobbes, that law was a command "prescribed by source superior and which the inferior is bound to obey"—such a sense of law as the declaration of a person or body existing independently above the subjects of law and imposing its will upon them, was brought into question by the developing notion of representation. Already in these years there were adumbrations of the sweeping repudiation James Wilson and others would make of Blackstone's definition of law, and of the view they would put in its place: the view that the binding power of law flowed from the continuous assent of the subjects of law; the view "that the only reason why a free and independent man was bound by human laws was this—that he bound himself."

These were deep-lying implications of making representation—systematically, in principle as well as in fact—"a substitute for legislation by direct action of the people." They were radical possibilities, glimpsed but not wholly grasped, thrown up in the creative clash of ideas that preceded the Revolution, and drawn into the discussion of the first state constitutions even before Independence was declared. They were perhaps, in these early years, understood most clearly by the more perceptive of the Tories, who stood outside and viewed with apprehension the tendency of events and the drift of theory. "The position," the Anglican minister Samuel Seabury wrote in 1774, "that we are bound by no laws to which we have not consented either by ourselves or our representatives is a novel position unsupported by any authoritative record of the British constitution, ancient or modern. It is republican in its very nature, and tends to the utter subversion of the English monarchy." . . .

In no obvious sense was the American Revolution undertaken as a social revolution. No one, that is, deliberately worked for the destruction or even the substantial alteration of the order of society as it had been known. Yet it was transformed as a result of the Revolution, and not merely because Loyalist property was confiscated and redistributed, or because the resulting war destroyed the economic bases of some people's lives and created opportunities for others that would not otherwise have existed. Seizure of Loyalist property and displacements in the economy did in fact take place, and the latter if not the former does account for a spurt in social mobility that led earlier arrivés to remark, "When the pot boils, the scum will rise." Yet these were superficial changes; they affected a small part of the population only, and they did not alter the organization of society.

What did now affect the essentials of social organization—what in time would help permanently to transform them—were changes in the realm of belief and attitude. The views men held toward the relationships that bound them to each other—the discipline and pattern of society—moved in a new direction in the decade before Independence.

Americans of 1760 continued to assume, as had their predecessors for generations before, that a healthy society was a hierarchical society, in which it was natural for some to be rich and some poor, some honored and some obscure, some powerful and some weak. And it was believed that superiority was unitary, that the attributes of the favored—wealth, wisdom, power—had a natural affinity to each other, and hence that political leadership would naturally rest in the hands of the social leaders. Movement, of course, there would be: some would fall and some would rise; but manifest, external differences among men, reflecting the principle of hierarchical order, were necessary and proper, and would remain; they were intrinsic to the nature of things.

Circumstances had pressed harshly against such assumptions. The wilderness environment from the beginning had threatened the maintenance of elaborate social distinctions; many of them in the passage of time had in fact been worn away. Puritanism, in addition, and the epidemic evangelicalism of the mid-eighteenth century, had created challenges to the traditional notions of social stratification by generating the conviction that the ultimate quality of men was to be found elsewhere than in their external condition, and that a cosmic achievement lay within each man's grasp. And the peculiar configuration of colonial politics—a constant broil of petty factions struggling almost formlessly, with little discipline or control, for the benefits of public authority—had tended to erode the respect traditionally accorded the institutions and officers of the state.

Yet nowhere, at any time in the colonial years, were the implications of these circumstances articulated or justified. The assumption remained that society, in its maturity if not in its confused infancy, would conform to the pattern of the past; that authority would continue to exist without challenge, and that those in superior positions would be responsible and wise, and

those beneath them respectful and content. These premises and expectations were deeply lodged; they were not easily or quickly displaced. But the Revolution brought with it arguments and attitudes bred of arguments endlessly repeated, that undermined these premises of the *ancien régime.*

For a decade or more defiance to the highest constituted powers poured from the colonial presses and was hurled from half the pulpits of the land. The right, the need, the absolute obligation to disobey legally constituted authority had become the universal cry. Cautions and qualifications became ritualistic: formal exercises in ancient pieties. One might preface one's charge to disobedience with homilies on the inevitable imperfections of all governments and the necessity to bear "some injuries" patiently and peaceably. But what needed and received demonstration and defense was not the caution, but the injunction: the argument that when injuries touched on "fundamental rights" (and who could say when they did not?) then nothing less than "duty to God and religion, to themselves, to the community, and to unborn posterity require such to assert and defend their rights by all lawful, most prudent, and effectual means in their power." Obedience as a principle was only too well known; disobedience as a doctrine was not. It was therefore asserted again and again that resistance to constituted authority was "a doctrine according to godliness—the doctrine of the English nation ... by which our rights and constitution have often been defended and repeatedly rescued out of the hands of encroaching tyranny ... This is the doctrine and grand pillar of the ever memorable and glorious Revolution, and upon which our gracious sovereign GEORGE III holds the crown of the British empire." What better credentials could there be? How lame to add that obedience too "is an eminent part of Christian duty without which government must disband and dreadful anarchy and confusion (with all its horrors) take place and reign without control"—how lame, especially in view of the fact that one could easily mistake this "Christian obedience" for that "blind, enslaving obedience which is no part of the Christian institution but is highly injurious to religion, to every free government, and to the good of mankind, and is the stirrup of tyranny, and grand engine of slavery."

Defiance to constituted authority leaped like a spark from one flammable area to another, growing in heat as it went. Its greatest intensification took place in the explosive atmosphere of local religious dissent. Isaac Backus spoke only for certain of the Baptists and Congregational Separates and against the presumptive authority of ministers, when, in the course of an attack on the religious establishment in Massachusetts, he warned that

we are not to obey and follow [ministers] in an implicit or customary way, but each one must consider and follow others no further than they see that the end of their conversation is Jesus Christ the same yesterday, and today, and forever more . . . People are so far from being under obligation to follow teachers who don't lead in this way they incur guilt by such a following of them.

It took little imagination on the part of Backus' readers and listeners to find in this a general injunction against uncritical obedience to authority in any form. Others were even more explicit. The Baptist preacher who questioned not merely the authority of the local orthodox church but the very "etymology of the word [orthodoxy]" assured the world that the colonists

have as just a right, before GOD and man, to oppose King, ministry, Lords, and Commons of England when they violate their rights as Americans as they have to oppose any foreign enemy; and that this is no more, according to the law of nature, to be deemed rebellion than it would be to oppose the King of France, supposing him now present invading the land.

But what to the Baptists was the establishment, to Anglicans was dissent. From the establishment in New England, ever fearful of ecclesiastical impositions from without, came as strong a current of anti-authoritarianism as from the farthest left-wing sect. It was a pillar of the temple, a scion of the church, and an apologist for New England's standing order who sweepingly disclaimed "all human authority in matters of faith and worship. We regard neither pope nor prince as head of the church, nor acknowledge that any Parliaments have power to enact articles of doctrine or forms of discipline or modes of worship or terms of church communion," and, declaring that "we are accountable to none but *Christ*"—words that had struck at the heart of every establishment, civil and religious, since the fall of Rome—concluded with the apparent paradox that *"liberty* is the *fundamental* principle of our establishment."

In such declarations a political argument became a moral imperative. The principle of justifiable disobedience and the instinct to question public authority before accepting it acquired a new sanction and a new vigor. Originally, of course, the doctrine of resistance was applied to Parliament, a nonrepresentative assembly 3,000 miles away. But the composition and location of the institution had not been as crucial in creating opposition as had the character of the actions Parliament had taken. Were provincial assemblies, simply because they were local and representative, exempt from scrutiny and resistance? Were they any less susceptible than Parliament to the rule that when their authority is extended beyond "the bounds of the law of God and the free constitution . . . 'their acts are, *ipso facto,* void, and cannot oblige any to obedience' " ? There could be no doubt of the answer. Any legislature, wherever located or however composed, deserved only the obedience it could command by the justice and wisdom of its proceedings. Representative or not, local or not, any agency of the state could be defied. The freeholders of Augusta, Virginia, could not have been more explicit in applying to local government in 1776 the defiance learned in the struggle with Parliament. They wrote their delegates to Virginia's Provincial Congress that

should the future conduct of our legislative body prove to you that our opinion of their wisdom and justice is ill-grounded, then tell them that your constituents are neither guided nor will ever be influenced by that slavish maxim in politics, "that whatever is enacted by that body of men in whom the supreme power of the state is vested must in all cases be obeyed," and that they firmly believe attempts to repeal an unjust law can be vindicated beyond a simple remonstrance addressed to the legislators.

But such threats as these were only the most obvious ways in which traditional notions of authority came into question. Others were more subtly subversive, silently sapping the traditional foundations of social orders and discipline.

"Rights" obviously lay at the heart of the Anglo-American controversy: the rights of Englishmen, the rights of mankind, chartered rights. But *"rights,"* wrote Richard Bland—that least egalitarian of Revolutionary leaders—"imply *equality* in the instances to which they belong and must be treated without respect to the dignity of the persons concerned in them." This was by no means simply a worn cliché, for while "equality before the law" was a commonplace of the time, "equality without respect to the dignity of the persons concerned" was not; its emphasis on

social equivalence was significant, and though in its immediate context the remark was directed to the invidious distinctions believed to have been drawn between Englishmen and Americans its broader applicability was apparent. Others seized upon it, and developed it, especially in the fluid years of transition when new forms of government were being sought to replace those believed to have proved fatal to liberty. "An affectation of rank" and "the assumed distinction of 'men of consequence' " had been the blight of the Proprietary party, a Pennsylvania pamphleteer wrote in 1776. Riches in a new country like America signified nothing more than the accident of prior settlement. The accumulation of wealth had been "unavoidable to the descendants of the early settlers" since the land, originally cheap, had appreciated naturally with the growth of settlement.

Perhaps it is owing to this accidental manner of becoming rich that wealth does not obtain the same degree of influence here which it does in old countries. Rank, at present, in America is derived more from qualification than property; a sound moral character, amiable manners, and firmness in principle constitute the first class, and will continue to do so till the origin of families be forgotten, and the proud follies of the world overrun the simplicity of the new.

Therefore, under the new dispensation, "no reflection ought to be made on any man on account of birth, provided that his manners rises decently with his circumstances, and that he affects not to forget the level he came from."

The idea was, in its very nature, corrosive to the traditional authority of magistrates and of established institutions. And it activated other, similar thoughts whose potential threat to stability lay till then inert. There was no more familiar notion in eighteenth-century political thought—it was propounded in every tract on government and every ministerial exhortation to the civil magistracy—than that those who wield power were "servants of society" as well as "ministers of God," and as such had to be specially qualified: they must be acquainted with the affairs of men; they must have wisdom, knowledge, prudence; and they must be men of virtue and true religion. But how far should one go with this idea? The doctrine that the qualifications for magistracy were moral, spiritual, and intellectual could lead to conflict with the expectation that public leaders would be people of external dignity and social superiority; it could be dangerous to the establishment in any settled society. For the ancient notion that leadership must devolve on men whose "personal authority and greatness," whose "eminence or nobility," were such that "every man subordinate is ready to yield a willing submission without contempt or repining"—ordinary people not easily conceding to an authority "conferred upon a mean man . . . no better than selected out of their own rank"—this traditional notion had never been repudiated, was still honored and repeated. But now, in the heated atmosphere of incipient rebellion, the idea of leaders as servants of the people was pushed to its logical extreme, and its subversive potentialities revealed. By 1774 it followed from the belief that "lawful rulers are the servants of the people" that they were "exalted above their brethren not for their own sakes, but for the benefit of the people; and submission is yielded, not on account of their persons considered exclusively on the authority they are clothed with, but of those laws which in the exercise of this authority are made by them conformably to the laws of nature and equity." In the distribution of offices, it was said in 1770, "merit only in the candidate" should count—not birth, or wealth, or loyalty to the great; but merit only. Even a deliberately judicious

statement of this theme rang with defiance to traditional forms of authority: "It is not wealth—it is not family—it is not either of these alone, nor both of them together, though I readily allow neither is to be disregarded, that will qualify men for important seats in government, unless they are rich and honorable in other and more important respects." Indeed, one could make a complete inversion and claim that, properly, the external affluence of magistrates should be the consequence of, not the prior qualification for, the judicious exercise of public authority over others. . . .

This was the ultimate concern. What . . . articulate defenders of the *status quo* saw as the final threat was not so much the replacement of one set of rulers by another as the triumph of ideas and attitudes incompatible with the stability of any standing order, any establishment—incompatible with society itself, as it had been traditionally known. Their fears were in a sense justified, for in the context of eighteenth-century social thought it was difficult to see how any harmonious, stable social order could be constructed from such materials. To argue that all men were equal would not make them so; it would only help justify and perpetuate that spirit of defiance, that refusal to concede to authority whose ultimate resolution could only be anarchy, demagoguery, and tyranny. If such ideas prevailed year after year, generation after generation, the "latent spark" in the breasts of even the most humble of men would be kindled again and again by entrepreneurs of discontent who would remind the people "of the elevated rank they hold in the universe, as men; that all men by nature are equal; that kings are but the ministers of the people; that their authority is delegated to them by the people for their good, and they have a right to resume it, and place it in other hands, or keep it themselves, whenever it is made use of to oppress them." Seeds of sedition would thus constantly be sown, and harvests of licentiousness reaped.

How else could it end? What reasonable social and political order could conceivably be built and maintained where authority was questioned before it was obeyed, where social differences were considered to be incidental rather than essential to community order, and where superiority, suspect in principle, was not allowed to concentrate in the hands of a few but was scattered broadly through the populace? No one could clearly say. But some, caught up in a vision of the future in which the peculiarities of American life became the marks of a chosen people, found in the de-

fiance of traditional order the firmest of all grounds for their hope for a freer life. The details of this new world were not as yet clearly depicted; but faith ran high that a better world than any that had ever been known could be built where authority was distrusted and held in constant scrutiny; where the status of men flowed from their achievements and from their personal qualities, not from distinctions ascribed to them at birth; and where the use of power over the lives of men was jealously guarded and severely restricted. It was only where there was this defiance, this refusal to truckle, this distrust of all authority, political or social, that institutions would express human aspirations, not crush them.

In the concluding essay GORDON S. WOOD raises some basic conceptual questions about the study of revolutionary ideology. Recall the points raised about Wood's article in the Introduction: his distinction between the idealist and behaviorist approaches to the study of political thought, his apparent call for a joining of the two, and his highlighting of the unconscious and irrational as well as conscious and rational dimensions of men's thought. As the reader follows the argument, he will want to think again about the various essays he has read, for Wood introduces new questions about the strengths and weaknesses of them all.*

Gordon S. Wood

Rhetoric and Reality
in the American Revolution

If any catch phrase is to characterize the work being done on the American Revolution by this generation of historians, it will probably be "the American Revolution considered as an intellectual movement." For we now seem to be fully involved in a phase of writing about the Revolution in which the thought of the Revolutionaries, rather than their social and economic interests, has become the major focus of research and analysis. This recent emphasis on ideas is not of course new, and indeed right from the beginning it has characterized almost all our attempts to understand the Revolution. The ideas of a period which Samuel Eliot Morison and Harold Laski once described as, next to the English revolutionary decades of the seven-

teenth century, the most fruitful era in the history of Western political thought could never be completely ignored in any phase of our history writing.

It has not been simply the inherent importance of the Revolutionary ideas, those "great principles of freedom," that has continually attracted the attention of historians. It has been rather the unusual nature of the Revolution and the constant need to explain what on the face of it seems inexplicable that has compelled almost all interpreters of the Revolution, including the participants themselves, to stress its predominantly intellectual character and hence its uniqueness among Western revolutions. Within the context of Revolutionary historiography the one

*From Gordon S. Wood, "Rhetoric and Reality in the American Revolution," *William and Mary Quarterly*, Series 3, XXIII (1966), 3–32. Footnotes omitted.

great effort to disparage the significance of ideas in the Revolution—an effort which dominated our history writing in the first half of the twentieth century—becomes something of an anomaly, a temporary aberration into a deterministic social and economic explanation from which we have been retreating for the past two decades. Since roughly the end of World War II we have witnessed a resumed and increasingly heightened insistence on the primary significance of conscious beliefs, and particularly of constitutional principles, in explaining what once again has become the unique character of the American Revolution. In the hands of idealist-minded historians the thought and principles of the Americans have consequently come to repossess that explanative force which the previous generation of materialist-minded historians had tried to locate in the social structure.

Indeed, our renewed insistence on the importance of ideas in explaining the Revolution has now attained a level of fullness and sophistication never before achieved, with the consequence that the economic and social approach of the previous generation of behaviorist historians has never seemed more anomalous and irrelevant than it does at present. Yet paradoxically it may be that this preoccupation with the explanatory power of the Revolutionary ideas has become so intensive and so refined, assumed such a character, that the apparently discredited social and economic approach of an earlier generation has at the same time never seemed more attractive and relevant. In other words, we may be approaching a crucial juncture in our writing about the Revolution where idealism and behaviorism meet.

It was the Revolutionaries themselves who first described the peculiar character of what they had been involved in. The

Revolution, as those who took stock at the end of three decades of revolutionary activity noted, was not "one of those events which strikes the public eye in the subversions of laws which have usually attended the revolutions of governments." Because it did not seem to have been a typical revolution, the sources of its force and its momentum appeared strangely unaccountable. "In other revolutions, the sword has been drawn by the arm of offended freedom, under an oppression that threatened the vital powers of society." But this seemed hardly true of the American Revolution. There was none of the legendary tyranny that had so often driven desperate peoples into revolution. The Americans were not an oppressed people; they had no crushing imperial shackles to throw off. In fact, the Americans knew they were probably freer and less burdened with cumbersome feudal and monarchical restraints than any part of mankind in the eighteenth century. To its victims, the Tories, the Revolution was truly incomprehensible. Never in history, said Daniel Leonard, had there been so much rebellion with so "little real cause." It was, wrote Peter Oliver, "the most wanton and unnatural rebellion that ever existed." The Americans' response was out of all proportion to the stimuli. The objective social reality scarcely seemed capable of explaining a revolution.

Yet no American doubted that there had been a revolution. How then was it to be justified and explained? If the American Revolution, lacking "those mad, tumultuous actions which disgraced many of the great revolutions of antiquity," was not a typical revolution, what kind of revolution was it? If the origin of the American Revolution lay not in the usual passions and interests of men, wherein did it lay? Those Americans who looked back at what they had been through could only marvel at the rationality and moderation, "supported by the energies of well weighed choice," involved in their separation from Britain, a revolution remarkably "without violence or convulsion." It seemed to be peculiarly an affair of the mind. Even two such dissimilar sorts of Whigs as Thomas Paine and John Adams both came to see the Revolution they had done so much to bring about as especially involved with ideas, resulting from "a mental examination," a change in "the minds and hearts of the people." . . .

The Americans, "born the heirs of freedom," revolted not to create but to maintain their freedom. American society had developed differently from that of the Old World. From the time of the first settlements in the seventeenth century, wrote Samuel Williams in 1794, "every thing tended to produce, and to establish the spirit of freedom." While the speculative philosophers of Europe were laboriously searching their minds in an effort to decide the first principles of liberty, the Americans had come to experience vividly that liberty in their everyday lives. The American Revolution, said Williams, joined together these enlightened ideas with America's experience. The Revolution was thus essentially intellectual and declaratory: it "explained the business to the world, and served to confirm what nature and society had before produced." "All was the result of reason. . . ." The Revolution had taken place not in a succession of eruptions that had crumbled the existing social structure, but in a succession of new thoughts and new ideas that had vindicated that social structure.

The same logic that drove the participants to view the Revolution as peculiarly intellectual also compelled Moses Coit Tyler, writing at the end of the nineteenth century, to describe the American Revolution as "preeminently a revolution caused by ideas, and pivoted on ideas." That

ideas played a part in all revolutions Tyler readily admitted. But in most revolutions, like that of the French, ideas had been perceived and acted upon only when the social reality had caught up with them, only when the ideas had been given meaning and force by long-experienced "real evils." The American Revolution, said Tyler, had been different: it was directed "not against tyranny inflicted, but only against tyranny anticipated." The Americans revolted not out of actual suffering but out of reasoned principle. "Hence, more than with most other epochs of revolutionary strife, our epoch of revolutionary strife was a strife of ideas: a long warfare of political logic; a succession of annual campaigns in which the marshalling of arguments not only preceded the marshalling of armies, but often exceeded them in impression upon the final result."

It is in this historiographical context developed by the end of the nineteenth century, this constant and at times extravagant emphasis on the idealism of the Revolution, that the true radical quality of the Progressive generation's interpretation of the Revolution becomes so vividly apparent. For the work of these Progressive historians was grounded in a social and economic explanation of the Revolutionary era that explicitly rejected the causal importance of ideas. These historians could scarcely have avoided the general intellectual climate of the first part of the twentieth century which regarded ideas as suspect. By absorbing the diffused thinking of Marx and Freud and the assumptions of behaviorist psychology, men had come to conceive of ideas as ideologies or rationalizations, as masks obscuring the underlying interests and drives that actually determined social behavior. For too long, it seemed, philosophers had reified thought, detaching ideas from the material conditions that produced them and investing them with an independent will that was somehow alone responsible for the determination of events. As Charles Beard pointed out in his introduction to the 1935 edition of *An Economic Interpretation of the Constitution,* previous historians of the Constitution had assumed that ideas were "entities, particularities, or forces, apparently independent of all earthly considerations coming under the head of 'economic.' " It was Beard's aim, as it was the aim of many of his contemporaries, to bring into historical consideration "those realistic features of economic conflict, stress, and strain" which previous interpreters of the Revolution had largely ignored. The product of this aim was a generation or more of historical writing about the Revolutionary period (of which Beard's was but the most famous expression) that sought to explain the Revolution and the formation of the Constitution in terms of socio-economic relationships and interests rather than in terms of ideas.

Curiously, the consequence of this reversal of historical approaches was not the destruction of the old-fashioned conception of the nature of ideas. As Marx had said, he intended only to put Hegel's head in its rightful place; he had no desire to cut it off. Ideas as rationalization, as ideology, remained—still distinct entities set in opposition to interests, now however lacking any deep causal significance, becoming merely a covering superstructure for the underlying and determinative social reality. Ideas therefore could still be the subject of historical investigation, as long as one kept them in their proper place, interesting no doubt in their own right but not actually counting for much in the movement of events.

Even someone as interested in ideas as Carl Becker never seriously considered them to be in any way determinants of what happened. Ideas fascinated Becker, but it was as superstructure that he enjoyed examining them, their consistency, their logic, their clarity, the way men formed and played with them. In his *Declaration of Independence: A Study in the History of Political Ideas* the political theory of the Americans takes on an unreal and even fatuous quality. It was as if ideas were merely refined tools to be used by the colonists in the most adroit manner possible. The entire Declaration of Independence, said Becker, was calculated for effect, designed primarily "to convince a candid world that the colonies had a moral and legal right to separate from Great Britain." The severe indictment of the King did not spring from unfathomable passions but was contrived, conjured up, to justify a rebellion whose sources lay elsewhere. Men to Becker were never the victims of their thought, always the masters of it. Ideas were a kind of legal brief. "Thus step by step, from 1764 to 1776, the colonists modified their theory to suit their needs." The assumptions behind Becker's 1909 behaviorist work on New York politics in the Revolution and his 1922 study of the political ideas in the Declaration of Independence were more alike than they at first might appear.

Bringing to their studies of the Revolution similar assumptions about the nature of ideas, some of Becker's contemporaries went on to expose starkly the implications of those assumptions. When the entire body of Revolutionary thinking was examined, these historians could not avoid being struck by its generally bombastic and overwrought quality. The ideas expressed seemed so inflated, such obvious exaggerations of reality, that they could scarcely be taken seriously. The Tories were all "wretched hirelings, and execrable parricides"; George III, the "tyrant of the earth," a "monster in human form"; the British soldiers, "a mercenary, licentious rabble of banditti," intending to "tear the bowels and vitals of their brave but peaceable fellow subjects, and *to wash the ground with a profusion of innocent blood.*" Such extravagant language, it seemed, could be nothing but calculated deception, at best an obvious distortion of fact, designed to incite and mold a revolutionary fervor. "The stigmatizing of British policy as 'tyranny,' 'oppression' and 'slavery,' " wrote Arthur M. Schlesinger, the dean of the Progressive historians, "had little or no objective reality, at least prior to the Intolerable Acts, but ceaseless repetition of the charge kept emotions at fever pitch."

Indeed, so grandiose, so overdrawn, it seemed, were the ideas that the historians were necessarily led to ask not whether such ideas were valid but why men should have expressed them. It was not the content of such ideas but the function that was really interesting. The Revolutionary rhetoric, the profusion of sermons, pamphlets, and articles in the patriotic cause, could best be examined as propaganda, that is, as a concerted and self-conscious effort by agitators to manipulate and shape public opinion. Because of the Progressive historians' view of the Revolution as the movement of class minorities bent on promoting particular social and economic interests, the conception of propaganda was crucial to their explanation of what seemed to be a revolutionary consensus. Through the use of ideas in provoking hatred and influencing opinion and creating at least "an appearance of unity," the influence of a minority of agitators was out of all proportion to their number. The Revolution thus became a display of extraordinary skillfulness in the manipulation of public opinion. In fact, wrote Schlesinger, "no disaffected

element in history has ever risen more splendidly to the occasion." . . .

With this conception of ideas as weapons shrewdly used by designing propagandists, it was inevitable that the thought of the Revolutionaries should have been denigrated. The Revolutionaries became by implication hypocritical demagogues, "adroitly tailoring their arguments to changing conditions." Their political thinking appeared to possess neither consistency nor significance. "At best," said Schlesinger in an early summary of his interpretation, "an exposition of the political theories of the antiparliamentary party is an account of their retreat from one strategic position to another." So the Whigs moved, it was strongly suggested, easily if not frivolously from a defense of charter rights, to the rights of Englishmen, and finally to the rights of man, as each position was exposed and became untenable. In short, concluded Schlesinger, the Revolution could never be understood if it were regarded "as a great forensic controversy over abstract governmental rights."

It is essentially on this point of intellectual consistency that Edmund S. Morgan has fastened for the past decade and a half in an attempt to bring down the entire interpretive framework of the socio-economic argument. If it could be shown that the thinking of the Revolutionaries was not inconsistent after all, that the Whigs did not actually skip from one constitutional notion to the next, then the imputation of Whig frivolity and hypocrisy would lose its force. This was a central intention of Morgan's study of the political thought surrounding the Stamp Act. As Morgan himself has noted and others have repeated, "In the last analysis the significance of the Stamp Act crisis lies in the emergence, not of leaders and methods and organizations, but of well-defined constitutional principles." As early as 1765 the Whigs "laid down the line on which Americans stood until they cut their connections with England. Consistently from 1765 to 1776 they denied the authority of Parliament to tax them externally or internally; consistently they affirmed their willingness to submit to whatever legislation Parliament should enact for the supervision of the empire as a whole." This consistency thus becomes, as one scholar's survey of the current interpretation puts it, "an indication of American devotion to principle."

It seemed clear once again after Morgan's study that the Americans were more sincerely attached to constitutional principles than the behaviorist historians had supposed, and that their ideas could not be viewed as simply manipulated propaganda. Consequently the cogency of the Progressive historians' interpretation was weakened if not unhinged. And as the evidence against viewing the Revolution as rooted in internal class conflict continued to mount from various directions, it appeared more and more comprehensible to accept the old-fashioned notion that the Revolution was after all the consequence of "a great forensic controversy over abstract governmental rights." There were, it seemed, no deprived and depressed populace yearning for a participation in politics that had long been denied; no coherent merchant class victimizing a mass of insolvent debtors; no seething discontent with the British mercantile system; no privileged aristocracy, protected by law, anxiously and insecurely holding power against a clamoring democracy. There was, in short, no internal class upheaval in the Revolution.

If the Revolution was not to become virtually incomprehensible, it must have been the result of what the American Whigs always contended it was—a dispute between

Mother Country and colonies over constitutional liberties. By concentrating on the immediate events of the decade leading up to independence, the historians of the 1950's have necessarily fled from the economic and social determinism of the Progressive historians. And by emphasizing the consistency and devotion with which Americans held their constitutional beliefs they have once again focused on what seems to be the extraordinary intellectuality of the American Revolution and hence its uniqueness among Western revolutions. This interpretation, which, as Jack P. Greene notes, "may appropriately be styled neo-whig," has turned the Revolution into a rationally conservative movement, involving mainly a constitutional defense of existing political liberties against the abrupt and unexpected provocations of the British government after 1760. "The issue then, according to the neo-whigs, was no more and no less than separation from Britain and the preservation of American liberty." The Revolution has therefore become "more political, legalistic, and constitutional than social or economic." Indeed, some of the neo-Whig historians have implied not just that social and economic conditions were less important in bringing on the Revolution as we once thought, but rather that the social situation in the colonies had little or nothing to do with causing the Revolution. . . .

In a different way Bernard Bailyn in a recent article has clarified and reinforced this revived idealistic interpretation of the Revolution. The accumulative influence of much of the latest historical writing on the character of eighteenth-century American society has led Bailyn to the same insight expressed by Samuel Williams in 1794. What made the Revolution truly revolutionary was not the wholesale disruption of social groups and political institutions, for compared to other revolutions such disruption was slight; rather it was the fundamental alterations in the Americans' structure of values, the way they looked at themselves and their institutions. Bailyn has seized on this basic intellectual shift as a means of explaining the apparent contradiction between the seriousness with which the Americans took their Revolutionary ideas and the absence of radical social and institutional change. The Revolution, argues Bailyn, was not so much the transformation as the realization of American society.

The Americans had been gradually and unwittingly preparing themselves for such a mental revolution since they first came to the New World in the seventeenth century. The substantive changes in American society had taken place in the course of the previous century, slowly, often imperceptibly, as a series of small piecemeal deviations from what was regarded by most Englishmen as the accepted orthodoxy in society, state, and religion. What the Revolution marked, so to speak, was the point when the Americans suddenly blinked and saw their society, its changes, its differences, in a new perspective. Their deviation from European standards, their lack of an established church and a titled aristocracy, their apparent rusticity and general equality, now became desirable, even necessary, elements in the maintenance of their society and politics. The comprehending and justifying, the endowing with high moral purpose, of these confusing and disturbing social and political divergences, Bailyn concludes, was the American Revolution.

Bailyn's more recent investigation of the rich pamphlet literature of the decades before Independence has filled out and refined his idealist interpretation, confirming him in his "rather old-fashioned view that the American Revolution was above all else an ideological-constitutional struggle and not primarily a controversy between social groups undertaken to force changes in the organization of society." While Bailyn's book-length introduction to the first of a multivolumed edition of Revolutionary pamphlets makes no effort to stress the conservative character of the Revolution and indeed emphasizes (in contrast to the earlier article) its radicalism and the dynamic and transforming rather than the rationalizing and declarative quality of Whig thought, it nevertheless represents the culmination of the idealist approach to the history of the Revolution. For "above all else," argues Bailyn, it was the Americans' world-view, the peculiar bundle of notions and beliefs they put together during the imperial debate, "that in the end propelled them into Revolution." Through his study of the Whig pamphlets Bailyn became convinced "that the fear of a comprehensive conspiracy against liberty throughout the English-speaking world—a conspiracy believed to have been nourished in corruption, and of which, it was felt, oppression in America was only the most immediately visible part—lay at the heart of the Revolutionary movement." No one of the various acts and measures of the British government after 1763 could by itself have provoked the extreme and violent response of the American Whigs. But when linked together they formed in the minds of the Americans, imbued with a particular historical understanding of what constituted tyranny, an extensive and frightening program designed to enslave the New World. The Revolution becomes comprehensible only when the mental framework, the Whig world-view into which the Americans fitted the events of the 1760s and 1770s, is known. "It is the development of this view to the point of overwhelming persuasiveness to the majority of American leaders and the meaning this view gave to the events of the time, and not simply an accumulation of grievances," writes Bailyn, "that explains the origins of the American Revolution."

It now seems evident from Bailyn's analysis that it was the Americans' peculiar conception of reality more than anything else that convinced them that tyranny was afoot and that they must fight if their liberty was to survive. By an empathic understanding of a wide range of American thinking Bailyn has been able to offer us a most persuasive argument for the importance of ideas in bringing on the Revolution. Not since Tyler has the intellectual character of the Revolution received such emphasis and never before has it been set out so cogently and completely. It would seem that the idealist explanation of the Revolution has nowhere else to go.

Labeling the recent historical interpretations of the Revolution as "neo-whig" is indeed appropriate, for, as Page Smith has pointed out, "After a century and a half of progress in historical scholarship, in research techniques, in tools and methods, we have found our way to the interpretation held, substantially, by those historians who themselves participated in or lived through the era of, the Revolution." By describing the Revolution as a conservative, principled defense of American freedom against the provocations of the English government, the neo-Whig historians have come full circle to the position of the Revolutionaries themselves and to the interpretation of the first generation of historians. Indeed, as a consequence of this historical atavism, praise for the contemporary or early historians has become increasingly common.

But to say "that the Whig interpretation of the American Revolution may not be as dead as some historians would have us believe" is perhaps less to commend the work of David Ramsay and George Bancroft than to indict the approach of recent historians. However necessary and rewarding the neo-Whig histories have been, they present us with only a partial perspective on the Revolution. The neo-Whig interpretation is intrinsically polemical; however subtly presented, it aims to justify the Revolution. It therefore cannot accommodate a totally different, an opposing, perspective, a Tory view of the Revolution. It is for this reason that the recent publication of Peter Oliver's "Origin and Progress of the American Rebellion" is of major significance, for it offers us—"by attacking the hallowed traditions of the revolution, challenging the motives of the founding fathers, and depicting revolution as passion, plotting, and violence"—an explanation of what happened quite different from what we have been recently accustomed to. Oliver's vivid portrait of the Revolutionaries with his accent on their vicious emotions and interests seriously disturbs the present Whiggish interpretation of the Revolution. It is not that Oliver's description of, say, John Adams as madly ambitious and consumingly resentful is any more correct than Adams's own description of himself as a virtuous and patriotic defender of liberty against tyranny. Both interpretations of Adams are in a sense right, but neither can comprehend the other because each is preoccupied with seemingly contradictory sets of motives. Indeed, it is really these two interpretations that have divided historians of the Revolution ever since.

Any intellectually satisfying explanation of the Revolution must encompass the Tory perspective as well as the Whig, for if we are compelled to take sides and choose between opposing motives—unconscious or avowed, passion or principle, greed or liberty—we will be endlessly caught up in the polemics of the participants themselves. We must, in other words, eventually dissolve the distinction between conscious and unconscious motives, between the Revolutionaries' stated intentions and their supposedly hidden needs and desires, a dissolution that involves somehow relating beliefs and ideas to the social world in which they operate. If we are to understand the causes of the Revolution we must therefore ultimately transcend this problem of motivation. But this we can never do as long as we attempt to explain the Revolution mainly in terms of the intentions of the participants. It is not that men's motives are unimportant; they indeed make events, including revolutions. But the purposes of men, especially in a revolution, are so numerous, so varied, and so contradictory that their complex interaction produces results that no one intended or could even foresee. It is this interaction and these results that recent historians are referring to when they speak so disparagingly of those "underlying determinants" and "impersonal and inexorable forces" bringing on the Revolution. Historical explanation which does not account for these "forces," which, in other words, relies simply on understanding the conscious intentions of the actors, will thus be limited. This preoccupation with men's purposes was what restricted the perspectives of the contemporaneous Whig and Tory interpretations; and it is still the weakness of the neo-Whig histories, and indeed of any interpretation which attempts to explain the events of the Revolution by discovering the calculations from which individuals supposed themselves to have acted. . . .

The neo-Whig "conviction that the colonists' attachment to principle was genuine" has undoubtedly been refreshing, and indeed necessary, given the Tory slant of earlier twentieth-century interpretations. It now seems clearer that the Progressive historians, with their naive and crude reflex conception of human behavior, had too long treated the ideas of the Revolution superficially if not superciliously. Psychologists and sociologists are now willing to grant a more determining role to beliefs, particularly in revolutionary situations. It is now accepted that men act not simply in response to some kind of objective reality but to the meaning they give to that reality. Since men's beliefs are as much a part of the given stimuli as the objective environment, the beliefs must be understood and taken seriously if men's behavior is to be fully explained. The American Revolutionary ideas were more than cooked up pieces of thought served by an aggressive and interested minority to a gullible and unsuspecting populace. The concept of propaganda permitted the Progressive historians to account for the presence of ideas but it prevented them from recognizing ideas as an important determinant of the Americans' behavior. The weight attributed to ideas and constitutional principles by the neo-Whig historians was thus an essential corrective to the propagandist studies.

Yet in its laudable effort to resurrect the importance of ideas in historical explanation much of the writing of the neo-Whigs has tended to return to the simple nineteenth-century intellectualist assumption that history is the consequence of a rational calculation of ends and means, that what happened was what was consciously desired and planned. By supposing "that individual actions and immediate issues are more important than underlying determinants in explaining particular events," by emphasizing conscious and articulated motives, the neo-Whig historians have selected and presented that evidence which is most directly and clearly expressive of the intentions of the Whigs, that is, the most well-defined, the most constitutional, the most reasonable of the Whig beliefs, those found in their public documents, their several declarations of grievances and causes. It is not surprising that for the neo-Whigs the history of the American Revolution should be more than anything else "the history of the Americans' search for principles." Not only, then, did nothing in the Americans' economic and social structure really determine their behavior, but the colonists in fact acted from the most rational and calculated of motives: they fought, as they said they would, simply to defend their ancient liberties against British provocation.

By implying that certain declared rational purposes are by themselves an adequate explanation for the Americans' revolt, in other words that the Revolution was really nothing more than a contest over constitutional principles, the neo-Whig historians have not only threatened to deny what we have learned of human psychology in the twentieth century, but they have also in fact failed to exploit fully the terms of their own idealist approach by not taking into account all of what the Americans believed and said. Whatever the deficiencies and misunderstandings of the role of ideas in human behavior present in the propagandist studies of the 1930's, these studies did for the first time attempt to deal with the entirety and complexity of American Revolutionary thought—to explain not only all the well-reasoned notions of law and liberty that were so familiar but, more important, all the irrational and hysterical beliefs that had been so long neglected. Indeed, it was the patent absurdity and implausibility of much of what the Americans said that lent credence and persuasiveness to their mistrustful approach to the ideas. Once this exaggerated and fanatical rhetoric was uncovered by the Progressive historians, it should not have subsequently been ignored—no matter how much it may have impugned the reasonableness of the American response.

No widely expressed ideas can be dismissed out of hand by the historian.

In his recent analysis of Revolutionary thinking Bernard Bailyn has avoided the neo-Whig tendency to distort the historical reconstruction of the American mind. By comprehending "the assumptions, beliefs, and ideas that lay behind the manifest events of the time," Bailyn has attempted to get inside the Whigs' mind, and to experience vicariously all of what they thought and felt, both their rational constitutional beliefs and their hysterical and emotional ideas as well. The inflammatory phrases, "slavery," "corruption," "conspiracy," that most historians had either ignored or readily dismissed as propaganda, took on a new significance for Bailyn. He came "to suspect that they meant something very real to both the writers and their readers: that there were real fears, real anxieties, a sense of real danger behind these phrases, and not merely the desire to influence by rhetoric and propaganda the inert minds of an otherwise passive populace." No part of American thinking, Bailyn suggests—not the widespread belief in a ministerial conspiracy, not the hostile and vicious indictments of individuals, not the fear of corruption and the hope for regeneration, not any of the violent seemingly absurd distortions and falsifications of what we now believe to be true, in short, none of the frenzied rhetoric—can be safely ignored by the historian seeking to understand the causes of the Revolution.

Bailyn's study, however, represents something other than a more complete and uncorrupted version of the common idealist interpretations of the Revolution. By viewing from the "interior" the Revolutionary pamphlets, which were "to an unusual degree, *explanatory*," revealing "not merely positions taken but the reasons why positions were taken," Bailyn like any idealist historian has sought to discover the motives the participants themselves gave for their actions, to re-enact their thinking at crucial moments, and thereby to recapture some of the "unpredictable reality" of the Revolution. But for Bailyn the very unpredictability of the reality he has disclosed has undermined the idealist obsession with explaining why, in the participants' own estimation, they acted as they did. Ideas emerge as more than explanatory devices, as more than indicators of motives. They become as well objects for analysis in and for themselves, historical events in their own right to be treated as other historical events are treated. Although Bailyn has examined the Revolutionary ideas subjectively from the inside, he has also analyzed them objectively from the outside. Thus, in addition to a contemporary Whig perspective, he presents us with a retrospective view of the ideas—their complexity, their development, and their consequences—that the actual participants did not have. In effect his essay represents what has been called "a Namierism of the history of ideas," a structural analysis of thought that suggests a conclusion about the movement of history not very different from Sir Lewis Namier's, where history becomes something "started in ridiculous beginnings, while small men did things both infinitely smaller and infinitely greater than they knew."

In his *England in the Age of the American Revolution* Namier attacked the Whig tendency to overrate "the importance of the conscious will and purpose in individuals." Above all he urged us "to ascertain and recognize the deeper irrelevancies and incoherence of human actions, which are not so much directed by reason, as invested by it *ex post facto* with the appearances of logic and rationality," to discover the unpredictable reality, where men's motives and intentions were lost in the accumulation and momentum of interacting events. The

whole force of Namier's approach tended to squeeze the intellectual content out of what men did. Ideas setting forth principles and purposes for action, said Namier, did not count for much in the movement of history.

In his study of the Revolutionary ideas Bailyn has come to an opposite conclusion: ideas counted for a great deal, not only being responsible for the Revolution but also for transforming the character of American society. Yet in his hands ideas lose that static quality they have commonly had for the Whig historians, the simple statements of intention that so exasperated Namier. For Bailyn the ideas of the Revolutionaries take on an elusive and unmanageable quality, a dynamic self-intensifying character that transcended the intentions and desires of any of the historical participants. By emphasizing how the thought of the colonists was "strangely reshaped, turned in unfamiliar directions," by describing how the Americans "indeliberately, half-knowingly" groped toward "conclusions they could not themselves clearly perceive," by demonstrating how new beliefs and hence new actions were the responses not to desire but to the logic of developing situations, Bailyn has wrested the explanation of the Revolution out of the realm of motivation in which the neo-Whig historians had confined it.

With this kind of approach to ideas, the degree of consistency and devotion to principles become less important, and indeed the major issues of motivation and responsibility over which historians have disagreed become largely irrelevant. Action becomes not the product of rational and conscious calculation but of dimly perceived and rapidly changing thoughts and situations, "where the familiar meaning of ideas and words faded away into confusion, and leaders felt themselves peering into a haze, seeking to bring shifting conceptions somehow into focus." Men become more the victims than the manipulators of their ideas, as their thought unfolds in ways few anticipated, "rapid, irreversible, and irresistible," creating new problems, new considerations, new ideas, which have their own unforeseen implications. In this kind of atmosphere the Revolution, not at first desired by the Americans, takes on something of an inevitable character, moving through a process of escalation into levels few had intended or perceived. It no longer makes sense to assign motives or responsibility to particular individuals for the totality of what happened. Men were involved in a complicated web of phenomena, ideas, and situations, from which in retrospect escape seems impossible.

By seeking to uncover the motives of the Americans expressed in the Revolutionary pamphlets, Bailyn has ended by demonstrating the autonomy of ideas as phenomena, where the ideas operate, as it were, over the heads of the participants, taking them in directions no one could have foreseen. His discussion of Revolutionary thought thus represents a move back to a deterministic approach to the Revolution, a determinism, however, which is different from that which the neo-Whig historians have so recently and self-consciously abandoned. Yet while the suggested determinism is thoroughly idealist—indeed never before has the force of ideas in bringing on the Revolution been so emphatically put— its implications are not. By helping to purge our writing about the Revolution of its concentration on constitutional principles and its stifling judicial-like preoccupation with motivation and responsibility, the study serves to open the way for new questions and new appraisals. In fact, it is out of the very completeness of his idealist interpretation, out of his exposition of the extraordinary nature—the very dynamism and emotionalism—of the Americans'

thought that we have the evidence for an entirely different, a behaviorist, perspective on the causes of the American Revolution. Bailyn's book-length introduction to this edition of Revolutionary pamphlets is therefore not only a point of fulfillment for the idealist approach to the Revolution, it is also a point of departure for a new look at the social sources of the Revolution.

It seems clear that historians of eighteenth-century America and the Revolution cannot ignore the force of ideas in history to the extent that Namier and his students have done in their investigations of eighteenth-century English politics. This is not to say, however, that the Namier approach to English politics has been crucially limiting and distorting. Rather it may suggest that the Namier denigration of ideas and principles is inapplicable for American politics because the American social situation in which ideas operated was very different from that of eighteenth-century England. It may be that ideas are less meaningful to a people in a socially stable situation. Only when ideas have become stereotyped reflexes do evasion and hypocrisy and the Namier mistrust of what men believe become significant. Only in a relatively settled society does ideology become a kind of habit, a bundle of widely shared and instinctive conventions, offering ready-made explanations for men who are not being compelled to ask any serious questions. Conversely, it is perhaps only in a relatively unsettled, disordered society, where the questions come faster than men's answers, that ideas become truly vital and creative.

Paradoxically it may be the very vitality of the Americans' ideas, then, that suggests the need to examine the circumstances in which they flourished. Since ideas and beliefs are ways of perceiving and explaining the world, the nature of the ideas expressed is determined as much by the character of the world being confronted as by the internal development of inherited and borrowed conceptions. Out of the multitude of inherited and transmitted ideas available in the eighteenth century, Americans selected and emphasized those which seemed to make meaningful what was happening to them. In the colonists' use of classical literature, for example, "their detailed knowledge and engaged interest covered only one era and one small group of writers," Plutarch, Livy, Cicero, Sallust, and Tacitus—those who "had hated and feared the trends of their own time, and in their writing had contrasted the present with a better past, which they endowed with qualities absent from their own, corrupt era." There was always, in Max Weber's term, some sort of elective affinity between the Americans' interests and their beliefs, and without that affinity their ideas would not have possessed the peculiar character and persuasiveness they did. Only the most revolutionary social needs and circumstances could have sustained such revolutionary ideas.

When the ideas of the Americans are examined comprehensively, when all of the Whig rhetoric, irrational as well as rational, is taken into account, one cannot but be struck by the predominant characteristics of fear and frenzy, the exaggerations and the enthusiasm, the general sense of social corruption and disorder out of which would be born a new world of benevolence and harmony where Americans would become the "eminent examples of every divine and social virtue." As Bailyn and the propaganda studies have amply shown, there is simply too much fanatical and millennial thinking even by the best minds that must be explained before we can characterize the Americans' ideas as peculiarly rational and legalistic and thus view the Revolution as merely a conserva-

tive defense of constitutional liberties. To isolate refined and nicely-reasoned arguments from the writings of John Adams and Jefferson is not only to disregard the more inflamed expressions of the rest of the Whigs but also to overlook the enthusiastic extravagance—the paranoiac obsession with a diabolical Crown conspiracy and the dream of a restored Saxon era—in the thinking of Adams and Jefferson themselves.

The ideas of the Americans seem, in fact, to form what can only be called a revolutionary syndrome. If we were to confine ourselves to examining the Revolutionary rhetoric alone, apart from what happened politically or socially, it would be virtually impossible to distinguish the American Revolution from any other revolution in modern Western history. In the kinds of ideas expressed the American Revolution is remarkably similar to the seventeenth-century Puritan Revolution and to the eighteenth-century French Revolution: the same general disgust with a chaotic and corrupt world, the same anxious and angry bombast, the same excited fears of conspiracies by depraved men, the same utopian hopes for the construction of a new and virtuous order. It was not that this syndrome of ideas was simply transmitted from one generation or from one people to another. It was rather perhaps that similar, though hardly identical, social situations called forth within the limitations of inherited and available conceptions similar modes of expression. Although we need to know much more about the sociology of revolutions and collective movements, it does seem possible that particular patterns of thought, particular forms of expression, correspond to certain basic social experiences. There may be, in other words, typical modes of expression, typical kinds of beliefs and values, characterizing a revolutionary situation, at least within roughly similar Western societies. Indeed, the types of ideas manifested may be the best way of identifying a collective movement as a revolution. As one student of revolutions writes, "It is on the basis of a knowledge of men's beliefs that we can distinguish their behaviour from riot, rebellion or insanity."

It is thus the very nature of the Americans' rhetoric—its obsession with corruption and disorder, its hostile and conspiratorial outlook, and its millennial vision of a regenerated society—that reveals as nothing else apparently can the American Revolution as a true revolution with its sources lying deep in the social structure. For this kind of frenzied rhetoric could spring only from the most severe sorts of social strain. The grandiose and feverish language of the Americans was indeed the natural, even the inevitable, expression of a people caught up in a revolutionary situation, deeply alienated from the existing sources of authority and vehemently involved in a basic reconstruction of their political and social order. The hysteria of the Americans' thinking was but a measure of the intensity of their revolutionary passions. Undoubtedly the growing American alienation from British authority contributed greatly to this revolutionary situation. Yet the very weakness of the British imperial system and the accumulating ferocity of American antagonism to it suggests that other sources of social strain were being fed into the revolutionary movement. It may be that the Progressive historians in their preoccupation with internal social problems were more right than we have recently been willing to grant. It would be repeating their mistake, however, to expect this internal social strain necessarily to take the form of coherent class conflict or overt social disruption. The sources of revolutionary social stress may have been much more subtle but no less severe.

Of all of the colonies in the mid-eighteenth century, Virginia seems the most settled, the most lacking in obvious social tensions. Therefore, as it has been recently argued, since conspicuous social issues were nonexistent, the only plausible remaining explanation for the Virginians' energetic and almost unanimous commitment to the Revolution must have been their devotion to constitutional principles. Yet it may be that we have been looking for the wrong kind of social issues, for organized conflicts, for conscious divisions, within the society. It seems clear that Virginia's difficulties were not the consequence of any obvious sectional or class antagonism, Tidewater versus Piedmont, aristocratic planters versus yeomen farmers. There was apparently no discontent with the political system that went deep into the social structure. But there does seem to have been something of a social crisis within the ruling group itself, which intensely aggravated the Virginians' antagonism to the imperial system. Contrary to the impression of confidence and stability that the Virginia planters have historically acquired, they seemed to have been in very uneasy circumstances in the years before the Revolution. The signs of the eventual nineteenth-century decline of the Virginia gentry were, in other words, already felt if not readily apparent.

The planters' ability to command the acquiescence of the people seems extraordinary compared to the unstable politics of the other colonies. But in the years before independence there were signs of increasing anxiety among the gentry over their representative role. The ambiguities in the relationship between the Burgesses and their constituents erupted into open debate in the 1750s. And men began voicing more and more concern over the mounting costs of elections and growing corruption in the soliciting of votes, especially by "those who have neither natural nor acquired parts to recommend them." By the late sixties and early seventies the newspapers were filled with warnings against electoral influence, bribery, and vote seeking. The freeholders were stridently urged to "strike at the Root of this growing Evil; be influenced by Merit alone," and avoid electing "obscure and inferior persons." It was as if ignoble ambition and demagoguery, one bitter pamphlet remarked, were a "Daemon lately come among us to disturb the peace and harmony, which had so long subsisted in this place." In this context Robert Munford's famous play, *The Candidates*, written in 1770, does not so much confirm the planters' confidence as it betrays their uneasiness with electoral developments in the colony, "when coxcombs and jockies can impose themselves upon it for men of learning." Although disinterested virtue eventually wins out, Munford's satire reveals the kinds of threats the established planters faced from ambitious knaves and blockheads who were turning representatives into slaves of the people.

By the eve of the Revolution the planters were voicing a growing sense of impending ruin, whose sources seemed in the minds of many to be linked more and more with the corrupting British connection and the Scottish factors, but for others frighteningly rooted in "our Pride, our Luxury, and Idleness." The public and private writings of Virginians became obsessed with "corruption," "virtue," and "luxury." The increasing defections from the Church of England, even among ministers and vestrymen, and the remarkable growth of dissent in the years before the Revolution, "so much complained of in many parts of the colony," further suggests some sort of social stress. The strange religious conversions of Robert Carter may represent only the most dramatic example of what was taking place less frenziedly else-

where among the gentry. By the middle of the eighteenth century it was evident that many of the planters were living on the edge of bankruptcy, seriously overextended and spending beyond their means in an almost frantic effort to fulfill the aristocratic image they had created of themselves. Perhaps the importance of the Robinson affair in the 1760's lies not in any constitutional changes that resulted but in the shattering effect the disclosures had on that virtuous image. Some of the planters expressed openly their fears for the future, seeing the products of their lives being destroyed in the reckless gambling and drinking of their heirs, who, as Landon Carter put it, "play away and play it all away."

The Revolution in Virginia, "produced by the wantonness of the Gentleman," as one planter suggested, undoubtedly gained much of its force from this social crisis within the gentry. Certainly more was expected from the Revolution than simply a break from British imperialism, and it was not any crude avoidance of British debts. The Revolutionary reforms, like the abolition of entail and primogeniture, may have signified something other than mere symbolic legal adjustments to an existing reality. In addition to being an attempt to make the older Tidewater plantations more economically competitive with lands farther west, the reforms may have represented a real effort to redirect what was believed to be a dangerous tendency in social and family development within the ruling gentry. The Virginians were not after all aristocrats who could afford having their entailed families' estates in the hands of weak or ineffectual eldest sons. Entail, as the preamble to the 1776 act abolishing it stated, had often done "injury to the morals of youth by rendering them independent of, and disobedient to, their parents." There was too much likelihood, as the Nelson family sadly demonstrated, that a single wayward generation would virtually wipe out what had been so painstakingly built. George Mason bespoke the anxieties of many Virginians when he warned the Philadelphia Convention in 1787 that "our own Children will in a short time be among the general mass."

Precisely how the strains within Virginia society contributed to the creation of a revolutionary situation and in what way the planters expected independence and republicanism to alleviate their problems, of course, need to be fully explored. It seems clear, however, from the very nature of the ideas expressed that the sources of the Revolution in Virginia were much more subtle and complicated than a simple antagonism to the British government. Constitutional principles alone do not explain the Virginians' almost unanimous determination to revolt. And if the Revolution in the seemingly stable colony of Virginia possessed internal social roots, it is to be expected that the other colonies were experiencing their own forms of social strain that in a like manner sought mitigation through revolution and republicanism.

It is through the Whigs' ideas, then, that we may be led back to take up where the Progressive historians left off in their investigation of the internal social sources of the Revolution. By working through the ideas—by reading them imaginatively and relating them to the objective social world they both reflected and confronted—we may be able to eliminate the unrewarding distinction between conscious and unconscious motives, and eventually thereby to combine a Whig with a Tory, an idealist with a behaviorist, interpretation. For the ideas, the rhetoric, of the Americans was never obscuring but remarkably revealing of their deepest interests and passions. What they expressed may not have been for the most part factually true, but it was

always psychologically true. In this sense their rhetoric was never detached from the social and political reality; and indeed it becomes the best entry into an understanding of that reality. Their repeated overstatements of reality, their incessant talk of "tyranny" when there seems to have been no real oppression, their obsession with "virtue," "luxury," and "corruption," their devotion to "liberty" and "equality"—all these notions were neither manipulated propaganda nor borrowed empty abstractions, but ideas with real personal and social significance for those who used them. Propaganda could never move men to revolution. No popular leader, as John Adams put it, has ever been able "to persuade a large people, for any length of time together, to think themselves wronged, injured, and oppressed, unless they really were, and saw and felt it to be so." The ideas had relevance; the sense of oppression and injury, although often displaced onto the imperial system, was nonetheless real. It was indeed the meaningfulness of the connection between what the Americans said and what they felt that gave the ideas their propulsive force and their overwhelming persuasiveness.

It is precisely the remarkable revolutionary character of the Americans' ideas now being revealed by historians that best indicates that something profoundly unsettling was going on in the society, that raises the question, as it did for the Progressive historians, why the Americans should have expressed such thoughts. With their crude conception of propaganda the Progressive historians at least attempted to grapple with the problem. Since we cannot regard the ideas of the Revolutionaries as simply propaganda, the question still remains to be answered. "When 'ideas' in full cry drive past," wrote Arthur F. Bentley in his classic behavioral study, *The Process of Government,* "the thing to do with them is to accept them as an indication that something is happening; and then search carefully to find out what it really is they stand for, what the factors of the social life are that are expressing themselves through the ideas." Precisely because they sought to understand both the Revolutionary ideas and American society, the behaviorist historians of the Progressive generation, for all of their crude conceptualizations, their obsession with "class" and hidden economic interests, and their treatment of ideas as propaganda, have still offered us an explanation of the Revolutionary era so powerful and so comprehensive that no purely intellectual interpretation will ever replace it.

Suggestions for Further Reading

The student seeking further reading on the methodological and conceptual problems of intellectual history should browse through the volumes of the *Journal of the History of Ideas* (1940–   ). Philip Wiener has gathered a number of the most important items originally appearing in this journal in a volume entitled *Ideas in Cultural Perspective* (New Brunswick, N.J., 1962).

Primary sources for the study of revolutionary political thought are abundant and relatively available in printed form. There are, first, the published works of numerous important revolutionary figures; in many cases modern and definitive editions are in process of publication. (For some of these, see below.) An extensive source collection, including most items published in the American colony/states before 1800, is Charles Evans, *American Bibliography*, 14 vols. (New York and Worcester, Mass., 1941–1959). Most of the material indexed in the Evans volumes has been reproduced on microcard. Bernard Bailyn is now editing a four-volume edition of *Pamphlets of the American Revolution* (1 vol. to date; Cambridge, Mass., 1965–   ). Other selected collections are by Merrill Jensen (ed.), *Tracts of the American Revolution* (Indianapolis, Ind., 1967); Samuel E. Morison (ed.), *Sources and Documents Illustrating the American Revolution, 1764–1788* (New York, 1923); and Jack P. Greene (ed.), *Colonies to Nation, 1763–1789* (New York, 1967).

Among general discussions of revolutionary ideology, special attention should be paid to two items. Gordon S. Wood, *The Creation of the American Republic, 1776–1787* (Chapel Hill, N.C., 1969) constitutes a major advance in our understanding of revolutionary political thought. It now stands as the single most important item

on the subject. Special attention also should be given to an article by Cecelia Kenyon entitled "Republicanism and Radicalism in the Revolution: An Old-Fashioned Interpretation," *William and Mary Quarterly*, Series 3, XIX (1962), 153–182. The revolutionary experience, she argues, was extraordinarily complex and involved a variety of ideological problems that developed at different rates and largely without common patterns.

In an essay, "Democracy and the American Revolution," *Huntington Library Quarterly*, XX (1956–1957), 321–341, Merrill Jensen suggests some of the ways in which the revolutionary experience worked to unsettle and open up political life and to radicalize patterns of American political thought. Taking a broader cultural perspective, Howard M. Jones explores the same subject in *O Strange New World* (New York, 1964). See especially Chapters 7 to 9 where he traces some of the far-reaching cultural implications of the revolutionary generation's republican orientation. In Chapter 7 of *American Minds* (New York, 1958), Stow Persons examines some of the central assumptions of the republican polity.

Among recent overviews arguing the conservative-legalistic-traditional character of revolutionary ideology, first mention should be given to Clinton Rossiter, *The Political Thought of the Revolution* (New York, 1963). See as well Benjamin Wright, "The Spirit of '76 Reconsidered," Chapter 1 in *Consensus and Continuity, 1776–1787* (Boston, 1958) and Thad Tate, "The Social Contract in America, 1774–1789: Revolutionary Theory as a Conservative Instrument," *William and Mary Quarterly*, Series 3, XXII (1965) 375–391. Daniel Boorstin, *The Genius of American Politics* (Chicago, 1953) stands somewhat by itself in asserting the starkly non-ideological character of the entire revolutionary movement.

In Parts 1 and 2 of *Seedtime of the Republic* (New York, 1953), Clinton Rossiter provides a useful examination of prerevolutionary political thought. See also Max Savelle, *Seeds of Liberty* (New York, 1948). Richard Buel analyzes patterns of political belief on the eve of revolution and finds them at most predemocratic in "Democracy and the American Revolution: A Frame of Reference," *William and Mary Quarterly*, Series 3, XXI (1964) 165–190. See also J. R. Pole, "Historians and the Problem of Early American Democracy," *American Historical Review*, LXVII (1962), 626–646. For an introduction to colonial society and politics generally, the reader should consult a companion volume to the present one in the American Problems Studies series: Michael G. Kammen (ed.), *Politics and Society in Colonial America* (New York, 1967).

For a careful examination of the constitutional issues between the colonies and England, see the following: R. G. Adams, *The Political Ideas of the American Revolution* (Durham, N.C., 1922); Charles H. McIlwain, *The American Revolution: A Constitutional Interpretation* (New York, 1923); and Edmund S. Morgan, "Colonial Ideas of Parliamentary Power, 1764–1766," *William and Mary Quarterly*, Series 3, V (1948), 311–341. Concerning the origins of American constitutional thought, see also Edward S. Corwin, *The 'Higher Law' Background of American Constitutional Law* (Ithaca, N.Y., 1955); Charles F. Mullett, *Fundamental Law and the American Revolution, 1760–1776* (New York, 1933); and Andrew C. McLaughlin, *The Foundations of American Constitutionalism* (New York, 1933). The major work on the Articles of Confederation is Merrill Jensen, *The Articles of Confederation* (Madison, Wisc., 1948). The related issue of civil liberties during the revolutionary era has been examined with quite different results by Zechariah Chafee, Jr. in *Free Speech in the United States* (Cambridge, Mass., 1948) and Leonard Levy, *Legacy of Suppression: Freedom of Speech and Press in Early American History* (Cambridge, Mass., 1960).

Another theme deserving mention concerns the role of propaganda in revolutionary political debate. Two works in particular deal directly with this problem: Philip Davidson *Propaganda and the American Revolution, 1763–1783* (Chapel Hill, N.C., 1941) and Arthur M. Schlesinger, *Prelude to Independence: The Newspaper War on Britain, 1764–1776* (New York, 1958).

Scholars have debated at length about the "sources" of America's revolutionary ideology. For a general treatment of the issue, see especially Chapter 2 of Bernard Bailyn, *The Ideological Origins of the American Revolution* (Cambridge, Mass., 1967) and Chapter 5 of Clinton Rossiter, *The Political Thought of the American Revolution* (New York, 1963). One of the specific questions involved in this discussion relates to the impact of the European Enlightenment on the American experience. Adrienne Koch in *Power, Morals and the Founding Fathers: Essays in the Interpretation of the American Enlightenment* (Ithaca, N.Y., 1961) argues that the influence of Enlightenment ideas upon American behavior was direct and determinative. Carl Becker, *Declaration of Independence: A Study in the History of Political Ideas* (New York, 1922) explains the deep importance of Lockian political theory. See also Part 2 of Stow Persons, *American Minds*, mentioned above, and Michael Kraus, *The Atlantic Civilization, Eighteenth-Century Origins* (Ithaca, N.Y., 1949). For the argument that the peculiarities of the American environment rather than ideas, enlightened or otherwise, lay at the heart of the American experience, see the various writings of Daniel Boorstin, especially: Chapter 3 of *The Genius of American Politics* (Chicago, 1953); "The Myth of an American Enlightenment," in *America and the Image of Europe* (New York, 1960); and *The Americans: The Colonial Experience* (New York, 1958). In an important essay, "Political Experience and Enlightenment Ideas in Eighteenth-Century America," *American Historical Review*, LXVII (1962), 339–351, Bernard Bailyn evaluates the relative importance of the two notions. Paul M. Spurlin examines *Montesquieu in America* (Baton Rouge, La., 1940).

Other intellectual traditions as well influenced revolutionary thought. Recently scholars have been emphasizing the political tradition deriving originally from republican Greece and Rome but more immediately from seventeenth- and eighteenth-century England. J. G. A. Pocock, "Machiavelli, Harrington, and English

Political Ideologies in the Eighteenth Century," *William and Mary Quarterly*, Series 3, XXII (1965) 549–583, focuses on the English scene. H. Trevor Colbourn, *The Lamp of Experience; Whig History and the Intellectual Origins of the American Revolution* (Chapel Hill, N.C., 1965) stresses the importance of republican historians. See also H. F. Russell Smith, *Harrington and His Oceana . . . and Its Influence in America* (Cambridge, England, 1914) and Oscar and Mary F. Handlin, "James Burgh and American Revolutionary Theory," *Massachusetts Historical Society, Proceedings*, LXXIII (1961), 38–57.

For information on the relevance of the classical tradition generally, see the earlier mentioned chapters of Jones, *O Strange New World*. Note also Richard Gummere, *The American Colonial Mind and the Classical Tradition* (Cambridge, Mass., 1963) and Charles F. Mullett, "Classical Influences on the American Revolution," *Classical Journal*, XXXV (1939) 92–104. The English common law tradition is examined by Charles F. Mullett in "Coke and the American Revolution," *Economica*, XII (1932) 457–471. A related topic is treated in Benjamin F. Wright, *American Interpretations of Natural Law* (Cambridge, Mass., 1931) and Ernest Barker, "Natural Law and the American Revolution," in *Traditions of Civility* (New York, 1948).

The character and function of religious belief in the revolutionary experience is a subject of considerable importance and difficulty. A great deal remains to be said about it. In the available bibliography, however, are several outstanding volumes. Note particularly Alan Heimert, *Religion and the American Mind, from the Great Awakening to the Revolution* (Cambridge, Mass., 1966), an extensive study of religious disputation and its political consequences in eighteenth-century American life. E. F. Humphreys, *Nationalism and Religion in America, 1774–1789* (Boston, 1924) seeks to explain the connections between these two phenomena. Alice Baldwin, *New England Clergy and the American Revolution* (Durham, N.C., 1928) is still useful. More recently, in *Mitre and Sceptre, Transatlantic Faiths, Ideas, Personalities, and Politics, 1689–1775* (New York, 1962), Carl Bridenbaugh has given careful consideration to the single most bothersome religious issue arising between

colonies and mother country—the question of establishing a colonial Anglican bishopric. Charles Akers' short biography, *Called unto Liberty: A Life of Jonathan Mayhew* (Cambridge, Mass., 1964) is suggestive.

Finally, the reader may wish to examine more closely certain leading revolutionary theorists. The following might serve as initial guides to further study. For James Madison, the chief primary source collection has been Gaillard Hunt (ed.), *Writings of James Madison*, 9 vols. (New York, 1900–1910). This is now being superseded by the modern and far more complete series, William T. Hutchinson and William M. E. Rachal (eds.), *The Papers of James Madison* (4 vols. to date; Chicago, 1962–   ). The standard biography is Irving Brant, *James Madison*, 6 vols. (Indianapolis, Ind., 1941–1961). Works dealing more directly with Madison's political thought include: Edward McNall Burns, *James Madison, Philosopher of the Constitution* (New Brunswick, N.J., 1938); Adrienne Koch, *Madison's 'Advice to my Country'* (Princeton, N.J., 1966); and Neil Riemer, "James Madison's Theory of the Self-Destructive Features of Republican Government," *Ethics*, LXV (1954–1955), 34–43.

The material on Thomas Jefferson is mountainous. For many years the 10-volume edition of Jefferson's *Writings*, edited by Paul L. Ford (New York, 1892–1899) was the best. Julian Boyd (ed.), *The Papers of Thomas Jefferson*, (12 vols. to date; Princeton, N.J., 1950–   ) will be definitive. Dumas Malone has completed three volumes (through 1800) of a projected multivolume biography, *Jefferson and His Time* (Boston, 1948–   ). Among other items see Daniel Boorstin, *The Lost World of Thomas Jefferson* (Boston, 1948); Charles Wiltse, *The Jeffersonian Tradition in American Democracy* (Chapel Hill, N.C., 1935); Adrienne Koch, *The Philosophy of Thomas Jefferson* (New York, 1943; and Julian Boyd, "Thomas Jefferson's Empire of Liberty," *Virginia Quarterly Review*, XXIV (1948), 538–554.

The once standard collection of Franklin's writings, in 10 volumes, was edited by Albert Smyth (New York, 1905–1907). A modern and complete version of Franklin's *Papers* is now being edited by Leonard Labaree (11 vols. to date; New Haven, Conn., 1959–   ). The best biography is still Carl Van Doren, *Benjamin*

Franklin (New York, 1938). An important book is Paul Connor, *Poor Richard's Politics: Benjamin Franklin and His New American Order* (New York, 1965). See also Malcolm Eiselen, *Franklin's Political Theories* (New York, 1928).

In the past, scholars have used the 10-volume set of the *Works of John Adams* (Boston, 1850–1856), edited by his grandson Charles Francis Adams. Here also a massive project is in progress under the editorial guidance of Lyman Butterfield, the goal, a definitive edition of Adams' writings. So far there have appeared four volumes of *John Adams' Diary and Autobiography* (Cambridge, Mass., 1961) and two volumes of *The Adams Family Correspondence* (Cambridge, Mass., 1963–   ). The most adequate biography is still Gilbert Chinard, *Honest John Adams* (Boston, 1933). For Adams' political thought, see Zoltan Haraszti, *John Adams and the Prophets of Progress* (Cambridge, Mass., 1952);

Edward Handler, *America and Europe in the Political Thought of John Adams* (Cambridge, Mass., 1964); and John Howe, *The Changing Political Thought of John Adams* (Princeton, N.J., 1966).

John Dickinson is treated in a recent biography by David Jacobson, *John Dickinson and the Revolution in Pennsylvania, 1764–1776* (Berkeley, Calif., 1965). For Joseph Galloway, see Julian P. Boyd, *Anglo-American Union: Joseph Galloway's Plans to Preserve the British Empire, 1774–1778* (Philadelphia, 1941). Charles Mullett has edited the political writings of James Otis in two volumes (Columbia, Mo., 1929). A sketch of Otis' life is available in Volume 7 of *Sibley's Harvard Graduates* (Boston, 1945). Frank Monaghan has written a useful biography of John Jay (New York, 1935). Charles Page Smith's biography, *James Wilson, Founding Father* (Chapel Hill, N.C., 1956) is quite good.